This book is being given to

_____

because I care about you and your family.

FAMILY EMERGENCY HANDBOOK

Three Steps to Protect Your Health, Wealth and Loved Ones

Cindy Arledge

Disclaimer

This book is sold with the understanding that the publisher and author are not engaged in rendering legal, accounting or psychological advice.

With the exception of the author's personal experiences, any similarity to actual people or places is coincidental. Names and places have been altered to protect confidentiality, and many stories are a compilation of actual experiences known to the author.

Every effort has been made to make this book as complete and accurate as possible. However, there may be mistakes both typographical and in content. Therefore, this text should be used only as a general guide.

The purpose of this book is to educate, empower, and inspire action. The author and Legacy Inheritance Partners, Ltd shall have neither liability nor responsibility to any person or entity with respect to any loss or damage caused or alleged to be caused directly or indirectly by the information contained in this book.

If you do not wish to be bound by the above, with proof of purchase, you may return this book to the publisher for a full refund.

Family Emergency Handbook:
Three Steps to Protect Your Health, Wealth and Loved Ones

Copyright © 2023 by Cindy Arledge

Published by: Legacy Inheritance Partners, Ltd
5100 Eldorado Parkway, Suite 102-703, McKinney, TX 75070

All rights reserved. No part of this book may be reproduced in any form or by any means, electronic or mechanical, including photocopying, recording or by any information storage system without written permission from the publisher, except by a reviewer, who may quote brief passages in critical articles or reviews.

The scanning, uploading, and distribution of this book via the internet or via any other means without the permission of the publisher is illegal and punishable by law. Please purchase only authorized electronic editions and do not participate in or encourage electronic piracy of copyrighted materials. Your support of the author's rights is appreciated.

ISBN: 978-0-9826953-8-8

Table of Contents

Introduction
Letter from Cindy Arledge ... 1
Inspiration ... 2
An Idea Was Born ... 3
Overview ... 4
Glossary of Terms ... 5
Supply List ... 6
Inner Circle and Ecosystem ... 7
Failing to Plan Is Planning to Fail ... 9
Outsmart Your Brain ... 10
Someday, the Day That Never Comes ... 11
The Frye Family Story ... 12
Find Your *Why* ... 34
Commitment Contract ... 35

Step One: Organize Your Legacy Drawer ... 37
Section 1: Medical Information ... 38
Section 2: Home ... 42
Section 3: Loved Ones ... 44
Section 4: Legal Documents ... 46
Section 5: Subscriptions and Security ... 49
Section 6: Bank Accounts and Credit Cards ... 51
Section 7: Assets ... 52
Section 8: Liabilities ... 54
Section 9: Insurance ... 55
Section 10: Personal Information ... 56
Section 11: End-of-Life Plan ... 57
Section 12: Communication Lists ... 60

Step Two: Create Your PEP Binder ... 62

Step Three: Train Your Team ... 63
Schedule Your PEP Plan Training Meeting ... 65
Maintaining Your PEP Plan ... 66
An Invitation ... 68

Appendix ... 69
Family Medical History ... 70
Home Contact List ... 71
Guest Instructions ... 72
Sample Guest Instructions ... 73
Home Maintenance Checklist ... 75
Sample Caregiving for Dependents ... 76
Sample Consent to Treat Dependents ... 77
Pet Record ... 78
Farm Animal Record ... 79
Farm Herd Record ... 80
Sample POA Pet Emergency Care ... 81
Sample POA Farm Animal Emergency Care ... 82
Vital Statistics ... 83
Advanced Planning and Final Instructions ... 84
Draft Obituary ... 86
Time Estimator Sheet ... 87
Unclaimed Assets ... 100
Preparing for the Will Conversation ... 101
Acknowledgments ... 102
Other books by Cindy Arledge ... 103
About the Author ... 104

Letter from Cindy Arledge

Dear Legacy Builder,

Congratulations! You are about to discover a secret that few families know.

I discovered it in my search for healing after my parents passed away 8 months apart in 2005. Despite my parents' elaborate estate plan, we paid $1,833,385.12 in estate taxes and spent years settling their estate. I refer to the years between my parents' deaths and the distribution of their estate as the *waiting room*.

My brothers and I lacked the skills to navigate the emotional storm of losing our parents while settling their estate. Lawsuits were filed and relationships were destroyed.

As a life-long learner I used the *waiting room* to understand what had happened to my family. I was surprised to discover 7 out of 10 families lose wealth during the inheritance process, and **97% of the time, wealth loss is caused by the family**.

In the process, I discovered how the wealthy stay wealthy. I refer to families who retain wealth for 100 years or longer as *Legacy Families* and vowed to share their secrets.

In this book you will discover one of the foundational legacy planning principles to help your family thrive. It's better to prevent a loss than need to recover from one. In other words...

Be ready. Life happens.

Being prepared for emergencies is a practical application of this secret. In this book you will learn three steps to create a Personal Emergency Preparedness Plan (PEP Plan) to eliminate **PREVENTABLE STRESS** for you and your loved ones.

What is PREVENTABLE STRESS? Stress that can be prevented through preparation. For example, spending hours looking for important documents. With your PEP Plan in place, your family will know exactly where your information is located, which will reduce their stress.

No amount of planning can eliminate all the stress that comes from death, end of life, chronic illness and other unexpected life events. By eliminating PREVENTABLE STRESS we free up time, energy and resources to deal with the stress that remains.

Congratulations, you're in the right place!

Cindy Arledge

Cindy Arledge, Certified Legacy Planning Advisor™

Inspiration

After my parents passed away, and while we waited for the IRS to accept the estate tax return, I discovered the following epitaph from the tomb of an Anglican Bishop (AD 1100) located in the crypts of Westminster Abbey.

> *When I was young and free and my imagination had no limits, I dreamed of changing the world. As I grew older and wiser, I discovered the world would not change, so I shortened my sights somewhat and decided to change only my country.*
>
> *But it, too, seemed immovable.*
>
> *As I grew into my twilight years, in one last desperate attempt, I settled for changing only my family, those closest to me, but alas, they would have none of it.*
>
> *And now, as I lie on my deathbed, I suddenly realize: If I had only changed myself first, then by example I would have changed my family.*
>
> *From their inspiration and encouragement, I would then have been able to better my country and who knows, I may have changed the world.*

This poem inspired the legacy planning process. The lesson I learned is when you want to change the world, start with yourself, *and then* change your family.

The legacy planning process will help you:

> **Design your significant life.**
> **Invite family participation.**
> **Co-create a better future.**

An Idea Was Born

"An ounce of prevention is worth a pound of cure."
— **Benjamin Franklin**

Life can change in a heartbeat. Literally. In one breath you can be fine, in the next breath not.

My daughters were in their mid-thirties when their dad, my ex-husband, had a stroke. A few days later, Tiffany, my eldest, gave birth to her third child in less than five years. Brittany, my youngest daughter, had two children under the age of nine.

In the middle of their already busy lives, without warning, or any preparation, the girls were making life and death decisions for their dad while managing all other aspects of his life.

In addition to taking care of his business and bills, they were also responsible for communicating with his bank, advisors, insurance companies and a host of medical professionals. And if that wasn't enough, they organized care for his herd of cattle located in the neighboring state of Oklahoma.

Thank goodness he had his will and estate planning done. The girls had the legal documents they needed to help their dad when he became incapacitated. They did an amazing job working together to help their dad throughout his recovery. The good news is, he has returned to work and resumed life without assistance.

From that crisis, I realized the ripple effect that occurs when supporting family members aren't prepared. The chaos increases exponentially.

The idea to create a family emergency plan was inspired by a news report about flooding on the Texas coast. A trained team of first responders showed up to minimize the effect of the storm and provide support to the community. I remember thinking, *wouldn't it be great if every family had their own trained team to show up and help in an emergency?*

I'd witnessed the impact on my daughters' lives when they became unpaid caregivers for their dad and decided to create something to make it easier for them to help me.

No parent wants to be a burden to their children. Everyone needs help at some point in life, so why not be proactive and make it easier to receive help?

Thus, the Personal Emergency Preparedness Plan was born.

After successfully implementing a plan for my family and helping clients implement a plan for their family, now it's your turn.

Overview

This handbook will show you how to create a loss prevention plan so that you are prepared for emergencies. When you create a Personal Emergency Preparedness Plan (PEP Plan), you can eliminate PREVENTABLE STRESS. While it is impossible to remove all the stress that comes with an emergency, it is possible to eliminate PREVENTABLE STRESS with a PEP Plan.

It's hard to think straight when you are feeling panicked. When you feel prepared, that panicky feeling goes away. A PEP Plan reduces stress, which empowers your family to remain clear, calm and confident to face life's unexpected events.

Create your PEP Plan by completing the following three steps:

1. ***Organize a Legacy Drawer*** so that your important documents are in one place and easy to find.

2. ***Create a PEP Binder*** to provide instructions to protect your health, weath and loved ones.

3. ***Train Your Team*** in advance by hosting a meeting to provide access to resources and co-create a response plan.

PEP Plan Steps:

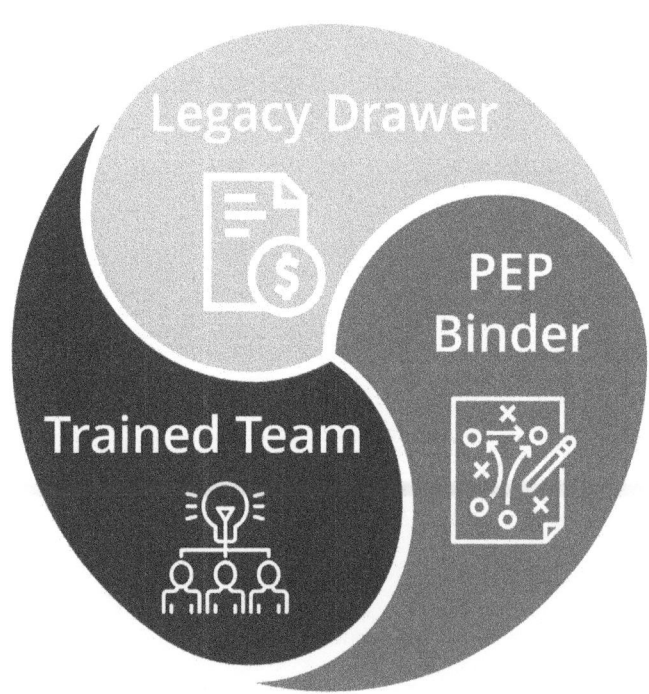

Glossary of Terms

PEP Plan: Personal Emergency Preparedness Plan. A three-part plan to (1) organize important documents, (2) create a resource binder with instructions in the event of an emergency, and (3) provide training for your team of family responders.

Legacy Drawer: Safe and secure location for important documents consisting of twelve sections.

PEP Binder: A portable resource binder of critical information that serves as an emergency loss prevention resource and a manual to train your PEP Team.

Inner Circle: The people you are consciously, or unconsciously, counting on to assist you when you need help. Your inner circle may include your spouse, family, friends, neighbors or business partners.

Ecosystem: The people who are counting on your help but are in no position to help you. Additionally, the inner circle of your inner circle.

PEP Team: Expanded group of support that includes business partners, neighbors, friends, family and professional advisors.

PEP Team Leaders: Trusted and available inner circle members who are capable of coordinating activities with your PEP Team when you become incapacitated or need help.

PEP Plan Training Meeting: Meeting for PEP Team Leaders to train them on the location of your Legacy Drawer, PEP Plan and to co-create a response plan.

Be Ready, Life Happens Workshop: Group training program for creating a Personal Emergency Preparedness Plan.

Supply List

This handbook has been written with the assumption that you will be creating a physical Legacy Drawer and a physical PEP Binder.* If you choose to follow these directions, you will need the following supplies to complete this project. If you don't have access to a computer or a printer with scanner, find someone who has one, and is willing to help you.

- 3-ring binder for your PEP Plan
- Dividers (five sections) for 3-ring binder
- Computer
- Printer with scanner
- Paper
- Filing cabinet or banker's box
- Files
- Labels
- Label maker
- Pen/pencil/sharpie
- Timer (You can use your phone, but don't let it distract you.)

*If creating physical files is a barrier for you to complete this project because you prefer a paperless system, create an electronic PEP Plan.

Inner Circle and Ecosystem

Before we get started on the details of the plan, it's important to identify who is in our inner circle and ecosystem.

We all have a mental list of people we are counting on should we need help. **This is your inner circle.**

Below is my inner circle. It includes my husband, two daughters, two brothers and my best friend.

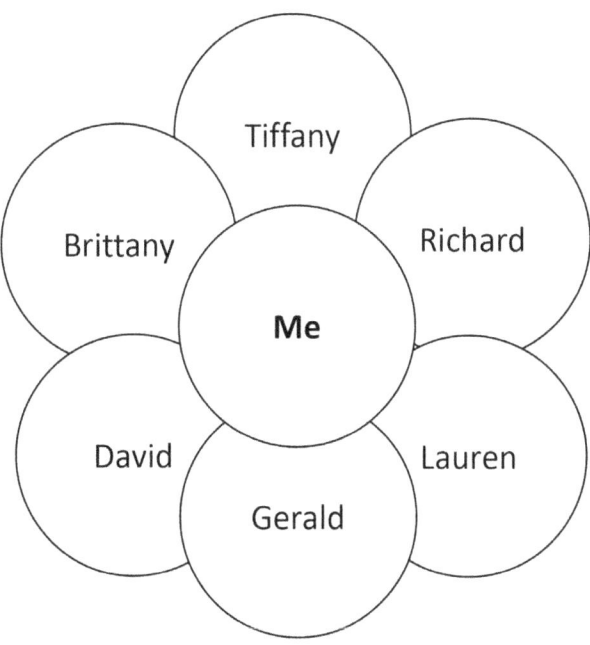

While my ex-husband and I have an amicable relationship and we attend lots of family events together, he isn't in my inner circle anymore.

But he is in my daughters' inner circle.

When he became temporarily incapacitated and my daughters became his informal caretakers, I stepped in to help them.

That's when I recognized that even though my ex-husband wasn't in my inner circle, he was in my ecosystem through my daughters' inner circle.

The people in your inner circle each have their own inner circle, which connects you to a wider group of people who have the potential to impact your life.

In addition, make a list of loved ones who are counting on you, but are in no position to help you, like an elderly aunt. Include them in your ecosystem.

Below is an example of my ecosystem.

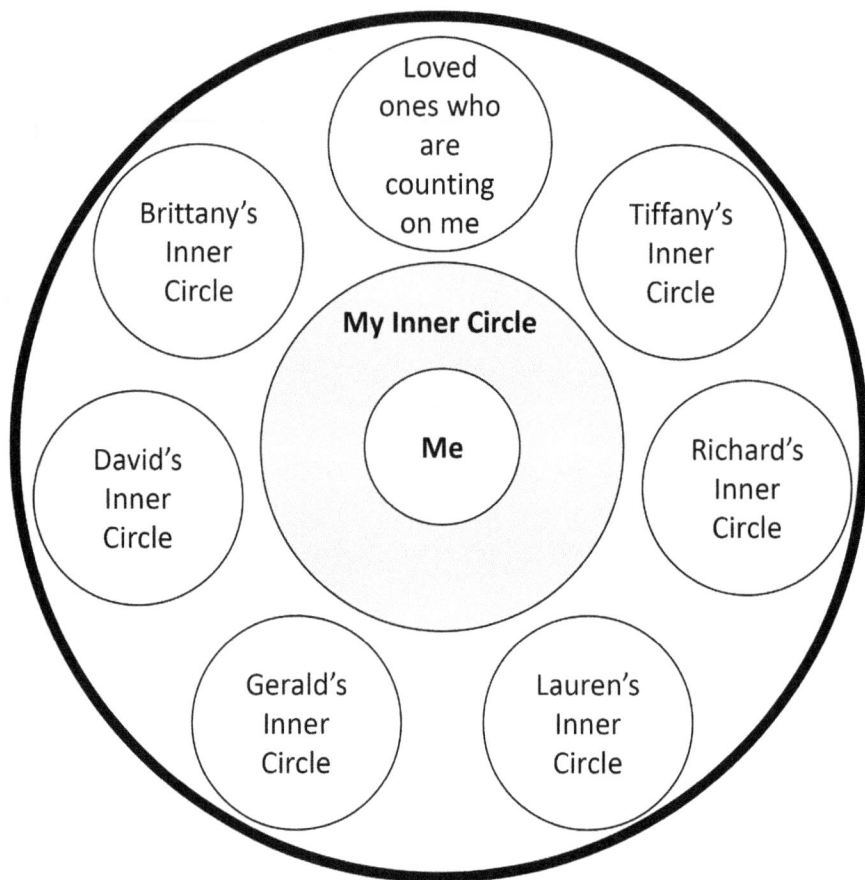

Action Steps:

1. **Make a list of the people in your Inner Circle.**

2. **Make a list of the people in your Ecosystem who are counting on you to help them. (When those in your Inner Circle identify their Inner Circle, you can add names to your Ecosystem.)**

Failing to Plan Is Planning to Fail

After leading countless families through this process in a variety of learning environments (three-hour workshop, 6-week course, digital online course, private one-on-one consulting) I've discovered a common theme.

> **Our lives are more complicated than we realize,**
>
> **and it takes longer to get organized than we think it will.**

The success rate for completing this project dramatically increased when clients had the opportunity to semi-accurately estimate the time commitment to organize their Legacy Drawer and create their PEP Binder. It will take longer than you think it will.

To make it easier to plan your time, I've included Time Estimator Sheets using the Pomodoro Technique in the Appendix. The Pomodoro Technique is a time-management method developed by Francesco Cirillo in the late 1980s. The Pomodoro Technique is a simple method that allows you to focus and stay mentally fresh by adding a small break between short work sessions that are called "pomodoro sessions."

To help you budget your time, each project has a time estimate for completion in pomodoro sessions of 30 minutes each. This includes 25 minutes to focus and a five-minute break before starting the next pomodoro-timed task.

Use the time estimator forms to create a time budget for completing this project.

Use the Pomodoro Technique to complete tasks by scheduling pomodoro sessions:

 Step 1. Pick a task.

 Step 2. Set a timer for 25 minutes and turn off all other distractions.

 Step 3. Stay focused on the task at hand until the timer goes off.

 Step 4. Take a 5-minute break.

 Step 5. Repeat as many times as your schedule allows with a longer break every two hours.

Creating a PEP Plan is an investment of time with a priceless ROI (Return on Investment of Time). You can't put a price on eliminating PREVENTABLE STRESS in advance. It's only when you are in the storm, overwhelmed and exhausted, that you recognize the peace and confidence that comes from being prepared.

Outsmart Your Brain

*"Courage is not the absence of fear,
it is the making of action in spite of fear..."*
— **M. Scott Peck**

You may be surprised to learn that your brain doesn't want you to complete a PEP Plan. Your brain is biased to put this project off.

In *The Ostrich Paradox: Why We Underprepare for Disasters*, authors Robert Meyer and Howard Kunreuther highlight six biases and how they affect our ability to prepare for potential disasters. The main focus of the book is disaster planning for natural disasters such as hurricanes, tsunamis, and flooding. These are low-probability occurrences with potential high costs that destroy homes and cause loss of life.

Ironically, these biases also apply to our ability to prepare for emergencies and death. Unlike low-probability occurrences, emergencies and death are *guaranteed* events in everyone's life.

If you don't have a will or estate plan, one or more of these biases has impacted you in the past. As you read the biases below, place a checkmark next to the ones you have experienced, or recognize may be a challenge for completing this project.

____ **Amnesia.** The tendency to forget lessons of the past.
Prince, the famed singer who passed away in 2016, didn't have a will.

____ **Herding.** The tendency to base choices on the observed actions of others.
Society, my family and friends don't talk about advanced planning, so I don't either.

____ **Optimism.** The tendency to underestimate the likelihood that a loss will occur.
"This won't happen to our family."

____ **Myopia.** The tendency to focus on short-term costs instead of seeing the long-term benefits. *"I'll do this later. I have more important things to do."*

____ **Inertia.** The tendency to take the path of least resistance.
I don't know what to do, so I won't do anything.

____ **Simplification.** The tendency to choose a subset of factors to consider.
"Even though 70% of families lose wealth during the first wealth transfer, it won't happen to us."

> **You are not your brain.**
> **Recognize these biases and outsmart your brain.**

Someday, the Day That Never Comes

"We are superior planners and inferior doers."
— Marshall Goldsmith

As someone who is dedicated to changing the herd bias, I talk about death all the time, even with total strangers! I use a rule I learned from Toastmasters International called *the three-foot-rule*.

Toastmasters International, an organization who helps its members overcome the fear of public speaking, use this rule to invite anyone within three feet to be a guest at a Toastmasters meeting so they can experience the benefits of membership. Although I am no longer a member, I use *the three-foot rule* to introduce Legacy Planning to complete strangers.

It was easy to use the three-foot rule as a Toastmaster because it was simply an invitation to attend our next meeting. Using *the three-foot rule* for legacy planning is much more personal. The lead-in question I use most is: *"Let me ask you a question. Do you have an updated will or estate plan?"*

I know it's a shocking question to ask a total stranger. This is by design.

People tend to remember our conversation because it is so direct, and they can see my sincere desire to help.

My family had to get over their embarrassment of me asking total strangers this very personal question. I ask waiters, the sprinkler repairman, my grandchildren's teachers, and literally anyone within three feet.

Most of the time, the answer to my question is: "No, not yet. I'll get to it someday."

Someday is a myth. *Someday* is a day too late.

Stop waiting for someday!

As you just learned, our brains are designed to delay emergency planning. Our brains urge us to wait for someday to keep those uncomfortable topics at bay. Ironically, our brains' biases which are designed to keep us "safe" actually *increase our danger*.

It doesn't help that our society supports the avoidance of addressing the topics of aging, death and money.

With these formidable obstacles in mind, there are two important steps you can take to successfully complete this process. Begin by finding a motivating *Why – why should I do this now?* Then make a commitment to yourself to complete the project.

Before you get started on your PEP Plan, I have a short fictional story to share with you.

The Frye Family Story

In this short, fictional parable, you'll follow Heather Frye, Ben Frye and their family as they journey through the 3-step process of putting together their PEP Plan. Afterwards, I'll take you through the steps to create your own PEP Plan.

Thursday, September 1st, 7:45 AM

Miles Corporate Headquarters

Heather Frye was distracted when she arrived at work. She felt deeply concerned about her stepson, Oliver. He was two weeks into his classes at TCU (Texas Christian University) and struggling, which meant the whole family was struggling. Oliver lived at home with the family on their small ranch north of Dallas three days a week. The rest of the time he rented a room close to campus from a fellow classmate.

Years ago, when Oliver was nine, his mom died from ovarian cancer. He was eleven when his dad, Ben, married Heather. Two years later, when Heather gave birth to fraternal twins, Mia and Mason, Oliver ecstatically welcomed his new half-siblings.

Oliver had always been patient and kind with the twins. But lately, he'd acted short tempered and snappish. *What's caused the sudden change in his behavior?* Heather wondered.

Heather entered the conference room where the other managers had already gathered. She was surprised to see Mary Fletcher sitting at the head of the table. Mary owned the company and normally didn't attend weekly team meetings.

Even in her distracted state of mind, Heather recognized an electric energy in the room. Putting aside her concern for Oliver, she focused on Mary. In addition to the other four managers sitting at the table, Mike, the CFO, looked like he had a delicious secret.

After everyone settled in, Mike started the meeting with a warm welcome and turned everyone's attention to Mary.

Mary said, "Five years ago, if you had asked me if Bob and I had done everything we could to protect our family's future, I would have naively answered, 'Yes.' We had an estate plan prepared by our attorney, our financial advisor managed our retirement plan, and our CPA took care of our accounting needs. We did everything we knew to do and patted ourselves on the back for a job well done." Mary sighed and shook her head. "When Bob died three years ago, I discovered *the hard way* that we weren't prepared after all. We didn't have a succession plan for the business. We didn't have an emergency plan for our family. And, I was unprepared for my role as his executor."

Mary paused to look around the table at her managers, then continued, "Last year, at the Dallas chapter Conscious Capitalism meeting, I met a Certified Legacy Planning Advisor™ and hired her to help me with my family."

Heather, who was in need of help with her family, was now suddenly curious. She spoke up, "Legacy Planning Advisor? I've never heard of that."

Mary looked down the table at Heather. "I didn't know what one was either, or Legacy Planning, for that matter. But after working with one, I learned that every family would benefit from adding a Legacy Plan to their planning effort. Legacy Planning is a little-known part of the estate planning industry that focuses on preparing the living."

"What do you mean *preparing the living*?" Heather asked.

Mary said, "After a loved one dies, family members who are left behind are often horribly unprepared to deal with the aftermath that follows."

Heather blinked. She wasn't comfortable thinking about death.

Mary continued, "There are many factors that can impact family relationships that lead to fighting over inheritances and control of the family business.

"Legacy Planning doesn't wait for a death to happen. The matriarch or patriarch of the family invites the entire family to participate while they are alive to resolve issues that could impact the family later.

"Legacy Planning is the secret ingredient for a thriving family. A Legacy Planning Advisor helps you get ahead of what is known as the Curse of Inheritance. The advisor I met with shared her insights and really opened my eyes to a new family model that's based on foundational principles. I have been impressed at the progress we've made. Instead of just being a parent, she showed me how to be a leader for my family. Instead of planning around my family, we invited them to participate. And instead of accidental success, our family now has a repeatable process that future generations can use long after I'm gone. I feel confident about our future for the first time since Bob passed away. And I discovered a whole new level of planning that I never knew was possible. The idea of creating a family emergency plan is based on the principle:

Be ready. Life happens.

"When I shared the process with Mike, he was fascinated and wanted to learn more, so I had my advisor call him. After meeting with her, Mike called me with a proposal. It sounded like a great idea, so here we are." Turning to Mike, Mary said, "Since this is your idea, I'd like you to lead the discussion."

All eyes in the room turned to Mike. Although he was the numbers guy, he was well liked and a champion of people. It didn't matter if you were the VP of Marketing or a machinist on the front line, he knew your name and always had a word of encouragement or a smile to share.

Mike said, "Mary has given her permission to initiate a 60-day pilot program for you, the management team, to implement a PEP Plan for your family.

If all goes well, we will roll the program out to the entire company."

He passed around binders titled *PEP Plan*. "Over the next two months, we want each of you to create a Personal Emergency Preparedness Plan, or PEP Plan for short, for your family."

Heather held her PEP Plan binder, wondering what all this involved. Would she and her husband actually talk about medical emergencies and *death*?

From a side table, Mike picked up a stack of books titled *Family Emergency Handbook* and handed one to every manager in the room. With a knowing smile, Mike said, "Your assignment is to read this book before our next one-on-one meeting. It's an easy read that you can complete quickly. Since Monday is Labor Day, we will meet on Tuesday. Thanks to Mary, and her support for this project, everyone who completes their PEP Plan by October 31st will receive a $1,000 bonus and an extra day of vacation."

Heather felt a surge of excitement through her chest. An extra $1,000 would be very helpful now that Oliver was in college. And an extra day of vacation would come in handy during the upcoming holiday season. She was totally on board.

Saturday, September 3rd, 8:00 AM

At home in the den, Heather pulled out her copy of the *Family Emergency Handbook* and settled into the cushy red chair overlooking the back pasture.

As she read through the introduction, her thoughts turned to her mom and her aunt. Heather's grandmother had died the month before. Heather remembered her mom saying, "Cleaning up MawMaw's house is a mess. I found her unpaid electric bill as a bookmark in the novel on her bedside table. I've spent hours looking for her life insurance policy, and I'm still looking for it."

Although the subject matter about death and emergency planning made Heather uncomfortable, she recommitted to finishing the book by the end of the day. She wanted to be ready for her one-on-one with Mike on Tuesday.

Forty-five minutes later, Heather put the book down on the table next to her chair. She was pleasantly surprised by how much she had covered in less than an hour. The content of the book was quite compelling. The next chapter was Section Four: Legal Documents, and she needed a break and more coffee before continuing.

Lost in thought, she poured the coffee too fast and was jolted back into the present by the steaming brown liquid spilling over the edge of her cup.

As she reached for the washrag in the sink, she grinned at the sign next to the sink.

"Always plan ahead. It wasn't raining when Noah built the ark."
— Richard C. Cushing

As she wiped up the spill, her thoughts returned to the task at hand. She wanted to finish the book today to understand the process so she could get started as quickly as possible.

Needing a break and not quite ready to tackle the next topic of legal documents, Heather sought out Ben. She knew exactly where he would be on a Saturday morning . . . in his shop.

As she entered his workshop, Ben looked up from a cabinet he was varnishing and said, "Hey, how's your day going?"

"So far, so good. Do you have a minute?"

Ben put down his paint brush. "Sure, this needs to dry anyway."

Heather explained, "I have an opportunity at work to earn a $1000 bonus and a day off."

"Wow, good for you! What do you have to do?"

After giving Ben a recap of the pilot program and what she had read so far, she said, "I'm excited to earn the bonus, but it seems like there will be a lot to do."

Heather gave him her most charming smile. "Will you be my accountability partner and help me with this project?"

Ben was hesitant. "My schedule is pretty busy, but I'm happy to help if I can. What do you need me to do?"

"I'm not sure yet. Let me finish the book and get some things in order over the weekend, then get back with you. Based on how much I've read, it looks like I can finish by lunch, then dive right into the activities."

Ben nodded and winked. "Looks like I've helped already."

As Heather turned to leave, Ben placed his hand on her arm. "I want you to know I appreciate the extra work you're doing and I'm happy to help anyway I can."

"Thank you, Ben. I'm going to multitask and read from the tub. Hopefully I can finish the book before I turn into a prune!"

Monday, September 5th, 7:30 AM

Kitchen Table

Heather shook her head as the sound of gunshots interrupted the peaceful quiet of the morning. Dove season had opened on September 1, and since it was Labor Day, there were more hunters than normal shooting on the neighbor's hunting lease.

When Heather moved to the ranch, she'd thought it would be quiet. But the noise of people, automobiles and sirens from living in the city had been replaced with the sounds of the wind through the trees, animals and gunshots. It was a trade she was happy to have made, except during dove season when hunters were hoping to bag their daily limit.

Ben set Heather's coffee cup on the table in front of her before settling into his chair. As steam curled up from their cups, Ben asked, "How is your work project going? What can I do to help you earn your bonus?"

Before answering, Heather took a small sip of coffee. "I finished the book on Saturday, and started going over my gameplan yesterday. I feel confident we can get the Legacy Drawer and PEP Binder done on time."

"Hold on, what are you talking about?" Ben said. "It sounds like you are talking in a foreign language. What is a Legacy Drawer and PEP Binder?"

"Oh, sorry. I've learned so much in such a short amount of time, and it makes so much sense to do. I hope you will take time to read the book so we can be on the same page," she said with a wink.

Ben groaned. "You and your puns."

She explained, "Basically, there are three steps to create a Personal Emergency Preparedness Plan, or PEP Plan for short.

"The first step is to organize important information into a file drawer. The author calls it a Legacy Drawer and it has twelve sections.

"The second step is to create a portable resource binder, or PEP Binder. It is created from the information you organize in your Legacy Drawer. As you organize and create documents you are actually doing the first two steps at the same time.

"The third and final step in the process is to create a team who can help you in an emergency and train them."

As Ben took all this in, he looked a bit overwhelmed. "That sounds like a lot of work."

"You know how my mom is struggling to settle my grandmother's estate?" Heather asked. "If my grandmother had done this process, my mom and Aunt Becky wouldn't be having such a hard time right now. I know this project sounds like a lot of work, but I believe getting all our affairs in order will help us in the long run. I'm hoping you will help me."

Ben nodded. "What kind of help do you need?"

"I need a place to set up our Legacy Drawer, and I was hoping you might have a spare drawer in your office we can use."

"I keep most of our personal records in the credenza behind my desk," he said. "You're free to use the file drawers on the right-hand side."

"Wonderful, thank you." Heather jumped up and gave her husband a hug. "I won't be creating a lot of new files, just rearranging our existing ones into twelve sections."

"Where are you going?"

"To your office to get started!"

Tuesday, September 6th

Miles Corporate Headquarters

After the holiday weekend, Heather returned to work and met with her boss, Mike, in his office. They caught up on company business, then Mike asked her for feedback on the PEP Plan.

Heather admitted, "I am excited and scared at the same time."

"What do you mean?" he asked.

"I read the entire book on Saturday and set up our Legacy Drawer files yesterday. My grandmother just passed away and my mom and aunt are having a terrible time. I don't want that scenario for my family so I'm excited to have a system to protect them. I even asked Ben to read the book and asked for his help."

"So, I'm confused. What's the problem?" Mike said with a laugh.

"After I set up the twelve sections, I used the time estimator sheets in the Appendix to calculate how long it will take us to complete the project. Yikes, it estimates that it will take 72.5 hours to complete the Legacy Drawer and PEP Binder. That doesn't include hosting a team meeting, that's just the time to organize the documents and create the binder. I don't know how we can get it done by the deadline." She sighed.

"Do you have the time sheets with you?"

"No, I didn't think I would need them today."

"First off, congratulations on the progress you made this weekend. You got a lot done and have much to celebrate. Remember what I learned from authors Dr. Ben Hardy and Dan Sullivan? Momentum is created from turning around to celebrate your gains, not measuring the gap between where you are now and the end goal. A ship never reaches the horizon.

"Mary and her family have their PEP Plan in place. Lucy and I finished ours last month. We have both been where you are. We wanted to see the management team's response before rolling it out to the entire company. I appreciate your enthusiasm. Do you have time in your schedule tomorrow to show me your time estimate sheets?"

"Sure, I can do that."

Mike nodded. "I am a resource to you and the other managers in the pilot program. If we decide to move forward with a company rollout, we want the managers to be a resource to help their teams."

After checking schedules, Mike and Heather decided to meet at 4:30 the next day.

That Night at Home

Ben was already in bed when Heather climbed in. She said, "My meeting with Mike went well today. He has already created a PEP Plan for his family so he may be able to help us save some time. He asked me to bring in our estimator sheets to go over them tomorrow."

"That's nice, honey," Ben said in a groggy voice.

Heather lay in bed with her supercharged brain spinning with ideas. She was eager for morning to come so she could get back to the office and discuss with her boss the best ways to conquer this challenge on time so she could earn her bonus.

Wednesday, September 7th, 4:30 PM

After initial pleasantries, Mike said, "Heather, I'm so glad you brought this up yesterday. The estimator sheets are in the Appendix for a reason. Most people don't even use them. They just start the process and don't worry about how long it will take.

The author recognizes everyone is different, and some people, like you, want the details before they begin. There is no right or wrong way to do this as long as it gets done. I found the estimates are overly generous, and think of them as a worst-case scenario."

"That's a relief," Heather said, "Maybe this won't take as long as I thought." She handed him her Time Estimator Sheet. "I made a copy of my time estimates for you."

Section	PEP Plan	Estimated Hours
Medical Information	Yes	15.5
Home	Yes	3.5
Loved Ones	Yes	7.0
Legal Documents	No	0.5
Subscriptions and Security	No	7.0
Bank Accounts and Credit Cards	No	2.0
Assets	No	5.5
Liabilities	No	5.0
Insurance	No	10.0
Personal Information	No	8.0
End-of-Life Plan	No	2.5
Communication Lists	No	6.0
Total Estimated Time		72.5

Mike took his time to review Heather's time sheet.

"Do you have experience using the pomodoro system?" he asked.

"No. I hadn't even heard of it before reading the handbook. Did you use it to complete your PEP Plan?"

"Yes, I did," he said. "I completed the project much faster than anticipated. The thirty-minute sessions helped my wife and I plan our time to get the project done. We worked as a team to complete the project and assigned different sections to each other. It was especially helpful in holding ourselves accountable. I'm curious to see if the leadership team has the same experience." He asked, "Do you mind sharing how you came up with these numbers?"

"Not at all," Heather said.

"Let's start with the Medical Section and see how far we get in the time we have scheduled."

Heather handed him a stack of printed pages. "I brought the Estimator Sheets for each section with me. Here are your copies. I really do want to do this for my family. Thank you for taking the time to review these with me."

#	Multiplied by	# of pomodoro sessions	Activity	Total Estimated # of Sessions
4	X	1	Family Medical History	4
5	X	2	Personal Medical History	10
5	X	1	Current Medical Condition	5
5	X	2	Medications & Supplements List	10
0	X	2	Medical Equipment & Supplies List	0
2	X	1	Health Insurance & Veteran's Benefits	2
3	X	2	Medical Contact List	6
			Total estimated pomodoro sessions:	37
			Divide the total pomodoro sessions by 2 to convert to hours.	÷ 2
			Total estimated hours to complete this section:	15.5

Mike said, "Please tell me how you calculated your pomodoro sessions and let's see if we can shave off some time."

"Ben has a son from a previous marriage, and we have twins together. We calculated we would need four separate family medical forms: one for Ben, one for me, one for Oliver and one for the twins. According to the book, we should plan on four pomodoro sessions to complete four forms, which is two hours."

"That looks right."

Heather continued, "We have five people who need a Personal Medical History, Current Medical Condition, and Medications and Supplements List, so that is fifteen forms. The estimate is 37 pomodoro sessions, or 15.5 hours!

"I have their shot records for school, but until this project I never thought about writing medical histories for my children. Mia had pneumonia as a baby and Mason broke his leg when he was two."

Mike said, "Lucy completed this part of the plan for us. She said the first form took the longest and once she got into the flow, it got easier and easier. I'll bet it won't take this long to complete these forms for your family."

"I hope you're right!" Heather said. "I'll start with the twins since they're the youngest. Ben can do his history, and I think it's a good idea to involve Oliver in this process. He can do his own. Maybe we can make it fun and do it together at the kitchen table with our favorite music playing. Afterwards, we can celebrate with a movie and popcorn with the twins."

Heather continued, "We don't have any medical equipment or supplies to list, which makes it easy. I wish my grandmother had created a PEP Plan. MawMaw had a walker, wheelchair, shower chair, portable toilet, bed lift, hospital bed and oxygen machine. It's taken my mom and Aunt Becky weeks to get everything sorted out. I know they would have been happy to help their mother get organized to avoid the nightmare they are going through now. This list alone would have saved them so much time and heartache.

"The company provides insurance for me and the children. Ben is a veteran and has veteran's benefits. We have 2 pomodoro sessions for this section. Ben can do his and I can do mine." Heather sighed, feeling better about the challenge ahead. "Thank you for walking me through the time sheet. I'm starting to see how I can delegate this work to Ben and Oliver. I don't have to do this all by myself."

Mike smiled, "That's right. And asking them for help means they are invested in the process."

Heather nodded. "We thought we could save some time by making one contact list for all three children since they see the same doctors. With that, we still have six pomodoro sessions, or three hours to create Medical Contact Lists for the family. Ugg, this sounds like a lot of work."

"Heather, you're right. It takes effort to do this planning. But let me ask you a question. Would you rather do it now, or be looking for this information in the middle of a crisis?"

"I don't want to do it during an emergency, that's for sure. I've already witnessed the chaos that my mom and Aunty Becky are dealing with."

"Well, it sounds like you understand the forms and how many you need. Are you ready to review the Home Section?"

"We have two houses," Heather said. "The one we live in and a rental property. My dad helped me buy out my ex-husband when we got divorced so I could stay in my house. When Ben and I got married, we decided to keep it as an investment. I'm repaying my parents with the rental income."

She continued, "After looking at the Home Maintenance Checklist in the Appendix, Ben and I thought it would be a good idea to invest the time to complete one for both properties. The time estimate for this section is 3.5 hours."

Mike said, "We liked the Home Maintenance Checklist, too. It's given us peace of mind to have a system for maintaining the house." He tapped the *Family Emergency Handbook*. "Did you see the advice to file your investment property files in the asset section?"

"Oh, I forgot about that. Thank you for the reminder."

"For the time we have remaining today, how about we review the Loved Ones section? Then we can schedule more time together."

Heather said, "In the Loved Ones Section, we have the twins, one dog, two horses and a herd of cows. Since Oliver is in college and an adult, I don't need to create a caregiving plan for him.

We didn't realize we couldn't make medical decisions for him or help him with his finances without legal documents. When Oliver turned eighteen we knew he was considered an adult. The school won't discuss his grades with us, but I didn't connect the dots of needing legal documents for him."

"It looks like your estimates are on target," Mike said. "Would you do me a favor and track your pomodoro sessions to your activities while you go through this process? The more information we can learn from the pilot program, the more information we can share when rolling it out to the entire company."

"I'm happy to do that. You know I'm a nerd for the details!"

Heather and Mike agreed to meet again on Friday at 3:00 PM.

That Night at Home

Ben spotted Heather heading for the back door, laden with groceries. She looked like a pack horse, so he rushed to open the door for her.

"I'd be happy to help relieve some of your burden," he said.

With a grin, she said, "That's OK. I enjoy the challenge."

As she put the groceries away, they talked about their day. Heather recapped her meeting with Mike.

"Wait a minute," Ben said. "It sounds like we don't need to use the estimator sheets but can still use the pomodoro sessions as a planning tool."

"That's a great idea, Ben. For most people that would work. But because I'm part of the pilot program, I agreed to track my actual time to my estimator time."

Friday, September 9th, 3:00 PM

Miles Corporate Headquarters

After reviewing the rest of her sections with Mike, Heather decided to leave the estimate as is.

"Mike, I'm curious… Why do you want everyone in the company to have a PEP Plan?"

"We learned from the COVID pandemic that it's impossible to ignore the millions of families who are struggling to survive in the U.S. and across the globe. We can't continue to pretend that our systems are working.

"Mary joined the Conscious Capitalism movement because she believes in the Conscious Capitalism philosophy that *business is a source of good*. According to the Conscious Capitalism website, 'Free enterprise capitalism is the most powerful system for social cooperation and human progress ever conceived.'"

Mike continued, "Success is more than the bottom line. It's one of four tenets of Conscious Capitalism. As a Conscious Capital company, we are committed to helping all our stakeholders."

"I've seen the benefits of that philosophy with our team," Heather said. "But now you're aiming to impact their families?"

He grinned. "Here's where it gets exciting. Legacy Planning recognizes *the family* as the smallest economic unit of society and is built on the philosophy that strong family units build strong communities. Strong communities build strong nations and strong nations lead to peaceful nations. Once I understood the similarities between Legacy Planning and Conscious Capitalism, I thought we could mesh the two together. We don't think about our team as individual people, we see them as families whose livelihoods are tied to our company's success. We believe there is great synergy in elevating humanity by adding Legacy Planning tools through the company to enhance our team's ability to thrive, and their families too."

"Mike, thank you for sharing this with me. By completing a PEP Plan, our family is getting economically stronger because we are implementing the principle: **Be ready. Life Happens**. When the people in my inner circle do the same, our entire ecosystem gets stronger."

Mike said, "I feel like we are part of a bigger movement. When more companies provide these tools to their teams, you can see how this will multiply throughout our community and beyond."

Saturday, September 10th, 8:30 PM

Ben Frye's Home Office

Ben had a will, but it hadn't been updated since his first wife passed away. Heather didn't have a will yet, and Oliver turned 18 on August 1, so he needed a will too. They would need three sets of documents. To earn her bonus, Heather planned to get their wills done through the legal service offered by the company. After pausing for a moment, she said with a heavy sigh, "I guess we should talk about getting our wills."

"Will we have time to get this done?" Ben asked.

"Maybe, I don't know. Let's start by having a conversation." Heather picked up the *Family Emergency Handbook* and opened it to the Appendix. "Let's review the *Preparing for the Will Conversation* and then look over the action list."

While Heather read the section out loud, Ben refilled their water bottles. Talking about wills was thirsty work.

After she was done, Heather suggested, "What do you think about doing two more pomodoro sessions now so we can get to bed at a decent hour?"

Ben agreed and reset the timer. He turned to the Legal section and made the following list.

1. Commit to a date.

2. Set a budget.

3. Decide who will write our documents.

4. Prepare for the meeting in advance.

"This may be easier than I expected," said Heather. "Why don't we commit to getting this done by the end of the month and use the legal services offered through the company? Three out of four, done! *Booyah!*"

Wincing, Ben said, "Hold on. I think we should talk about this. Oliver has a trust that was established when his mom died. Maybe we should use an attorney?"

Knowing how sensitive Ben was about his son, Heather took a deep breath and said in a soothing tone, "Hmm, I hadn't thought about that. Do you have someone in mind?"

Ben responded in a calmer voice, "Thank you for understanding. Let me talk with the attorney that set up the trust. I have her contact information in the file."

"Of course. This is an emotional topic. One we haven't tackled before. By getting started now, we have time to explore our options."

As Ben was stopping the timer on his phone, Heather reached over and put her hand on his. When he looked up, she smiled and said, "Thank you for our family. Thank you for the life we are building. Thank you for always supporting me."

Ben laid down the phone and gathered Heather's delicate hand between his huge hands.

After a beat, he said, "Thank you, as well. When Oliver's mother died, I didn't know if I would ever love again. You coming into my life was truly a gift. You opened my heart. You are a wonderful partner and mother to the twins. And I appreciate how you love Oliver as if he was your own." Ben sighed, then said, "I am committed to getting this project done because I can see how helpful it will be in an emergency. When Lisa was sick, everything was a struggle. I was totally unprepared. In addition to worrying about Lisa, I was trying to take care of Oliver and maintain our household without her. I could barely function. We were in a constant state of stress and chaos. When the doctors needed medical information for Lisa, I struggled to find it. After she passed, my struggles continued. Our finances were a mess, because Lisa had done the bookkeeping, and I didn't know where she kept our records. I didn't know her usernames and passwords. It was a nightmare."

Ben's face looked pained as he shared. "Oliver suffered too, because not only was he grieving for his mother, I was stressed all the time. Even though I was doing the best I could, I was barely keeping my head above water. I wasn't there for him as much as he needed me to be."

Ben looked out the window a moment, then back at Heather. "Now, I know it's not a matter of *if*, but *when* the next crisis happens. Our parents are getting older. Aunt Jenny is going downhill fast. I can't believe Oliver started college already. I'm grateful that Mary has given us these tools. It's just common sense to be prepared for emergencies."

Heather teared up, grateful that Ben was on board with creating their emergency plan together. He had never talked about the tough times he had endured after Lisa's death. Heather was touched by his willingness to be vulnerable and surprised that this conversation, the one she had been dreading, had made it happen.

Ben and Heather spent the remaining time discussing their wills. When the timer for the second pomodoro session dinged that time was up, they felt better. There were plenty of tasks left to do, but they had at least set a deadline to have their wills done.

Commitment to Obtain Will

Ben – October 14

Heather – October 14

Oliver – October 14

Saturday, September 17th, 6:30 PM

Frye Family Kitchen

Heather was amazed how each pomodoro session got easier and easier to complete. Momentum grew with every document she created and filed. With each section that was completed, Heather's confidence grew about their ability to be prepared for emergencies.

As an added benefit, they got a big-picture look at their finances and how disorganized their accounts and files really were. They came up with a more efficient system of keeping important records and found several online subscriptions they were paying for and didn't even use. Cancelling subscriptions was like finding money.

As Oliver was getting up to put his dishes in the sink, Ben asked, "Oliver, now that you're eighteen, we need to set up an appointment with an attorney to get you a will and other legal documents."

"I don't want to go!" Oliver screamed and ran out the door.

Startled, Ben and Heather looked at each other in confusion.

Angry, Ben jumped up to follow Oliver, but Heather stopped him. "Ben, have you noticed that Oliver hasn't been himself since school started?"

"Not really. I've haven't seen very much of him. He's either gone, or in his room."

"Well, I've been worried about him for weeks. I haven't said anything because I was hoping he would snap out of his funk. He's been grumpy with the twins, which isn't like him. What do you think is going on?"

With a heavy sigh, Ben said, "I'm not sure, but I suspect it has something to do with his mom. Let me talk to him and see if I can find out."

Saturday, September 17th, 6:45 PM

As Ben entered the horse barn, he could hear sobs coming from the end stall on the right. Light puffs of dirt floated like sifted flour with each step he took. When he opened the latch to the stall, he found Oliver hunched down in the hay in the corner. His arms were wrapped around his legs, his head resting on his knees.

Ben sat down next to his son and didn't say a word.

After a few minutes, Oliver's breathing smoothed out and without looking up, he said, "I know I was out of line tonight. I'm sorry, Dad."

Ben laid an arm over his son's shoulders. "Apology accepted. I'm worried about you, son. You're not yourself. Is there anything I can do to help?"

"Not tonight. I just need some time to think."

"I understand." Ben removed his arm from around Oliver's shoulders and settled in the hay next to him. Ben leaned against the rough wood as if it were perfectly normal for them to be sitting together in a horse stall.

"Dad? What are you doing?"

"Being here for you."

"I don't want to talk about this tonight."

"I'm not asking you to, son."

"Aren't you mad at me for screaming and running out the door?"

"I was at first, then Heather helped me realize that you were hurting."

"I said, I don't want to talk tonight."

"OK."

After several minutes of silence, with a quiver in his voice, Oliver whispered, "I miss Mom. TCU was her school, and now that I'm there, I miss her more than ever. I'm walking the same halls she walked, and I realize I don't know who she was outside of being my mom. My memories of her are of her being sick."

Oliver hung his head over his arms and began sobbing again. Ben leaned over and hugged his son. They cried together until there were no more tears to shed.

Saturday, September 17th, 8:30 PM

After regaining his composure, Ben asked Oliver to come to his office. As Oliver sat in the chair across from the desk, Ben pulled a banker's box from the top shelf of his security closet and put it on his desk.

As he looked into Oliver's questioning eyes, Ben said, "I've been saving this box for you since your mom passed away. I didn't know when to give it to you, and tonight seems like the right time. You have grown up to be exactly the man your mom wanted you to become. She would be so happy to know you are going to her alma mater."

For a beat, Ben's hand rested on top of the box. "This box has your mother's journals and photos. Please feel free to ask me any questions about her. And I know your grandparents would be happy to talk with you about her as well. We all miss your mom."

As Ben talked, fresh tears began flowing down Oliver's cheeks. He croaked out, "Thanks Dad, I'll take this to my room."

Sunday, September 18th, 7:30 AM

The next morning, Oliver seemed like a new person. He had a bounce to his step. He even volunteered to help the twins feed and groom the horses.

Heather raised her eyebrows at Ben and they both smiled.

"Can we talk about our PEP Team this morning?" Heather asked. "I want to decide who we should invite and pick a date and time to host our PEP Plan training meeting. How about Saturday, October 22nd? It won't interfere with Halloween, and we can get it done by the deadline."

"I'm still not sure how to do this," Ben said.

"Me neither, which is why I am glad we have the handbook."

She turned to the Glossary of Terms page. "It looks like we need to identify our PEP Team first. From that list we identify PEP Team Leaders. Then, we host a meeting for our PEP Team Leaders who we are counting on to help. We can show them where our Legacy Drawer is located. We need to decide if we are going to give them a copy of our PEP Binder or show them where it's kept, and co-create a response plan. What I like the most is expressing our gratitude."

"Please remind me again," Ben said. "What does PEP stand for, and who do we want on our PEP Team?"

"PEP is an acronym for Personal Emergency Preparedness." Heather read the definition of a PEP Team from the handbook's glossary:

> "**PEP Team:** *Expanded group of support that includes business partners, neighbors, friends, family and professional advisors.*"

Ben and Heather started by making a list of friends and family members who had helped them in the past.

Once they had this list together, they talked about their advisors and others who might help to add to their team. Ben's good friend would help him with his business, and Mike and Heather's assistant would be her contacts from work.

From the PEP Team contact list, they talked about who to invite to the PEP Plan training meeting.

Ben's mom was retired and had the time and heart to take care of the children. Oliver was old enough to take care of the animals, If he was too busy with school, they could ask their neighbor to help.

Heather and Ben would be each other's backup for bill paying. If they needed outside help, Heather's dad would be a good choice to protect their finances.

In the end, for their PEP Plan training meeting, they settled on inviting Ben's parents, Heather's parents, and the neighbor next door. They decided to serve spaghetti and Heather would make her signature cheesecake.

Their parents would arrive at noon to go over the Legacy Drawer and PEP Binder. The neighbor was invited to come at 1:00 for lunch and conversation.

There was some debate about whether to invite Ben's deceased wife's parents. They spent time with Oliver by taking him on occasional trips in their motor home. Since they traveled so much and hadn't spent much time with Heather or the twins, Ben and Heather decided to not include Lisa's parents in the meeting.

There was also a conversation about whether Oliver and the twins should participate. Growing up on the ranch and being responsible for their animals had helped them become mature for their age. In the end, Heather and Ben decided to include them all. The sooner they were exposed to this level of preparation, the better.

Friday, October 14th, 1:00 PM

As Heather, Ben and Oliver entered the attorney's office they were warmly greeted.

"I'm so happy to see you," their attorney, Blanche Holbrook said. "So few families realize the importance of legal documents and fail to include young adults into the discussion. Please find a seat in the conference room while I get two witnesses and the notary to join us."

In less than an hour, Heather, Ben and Oliver had updated legal documents. The attorney provided them with a digital copy on a jump drive as well as original documents.

"That's it?" Heather asked.

"You're all set," Blanche said.

"Wow, that was anticlimactic." Oliver said with a laugh.

Ben said, "Well, we did all the hard work last week reviewing the paperwork and asking questions."

As they were leaving the attorney's office, Heather said, "Let's celebrate! Anyone up for ice cream?"

Saturday, October 22nd, Noon
PEP Plan Training Meeting

The den was crowded like Christmas morning. Ben's parents and Oliver were parked on the couch. Heather's parents took the love seat. The twins sat on the floor. Ben and Heather perched on the fireplace.

In preparation for the meeting, Heather had purchased six copies of the *Family Emergency Handbook* and three binders. She made copies of their PEP Plan and put them in the binders as well as the contact list for their PEP Team.

After everyone was settled, Heather looked around the room. It was filled with the people she loved the most. "Welcome, everyone. Thank you for coming. When Ben and I needed help in the past, you were always there for us, and we are grateful for your support. I was recently challenged at work to take our planning to the next level by creating a Personal Emergency Preparedness Plan. Mom, you know how hard it's been to take care of MawMaw's stuff. We are excited to share our plan with you to reduce UNNECESSARY STRESS."

After Heather explained how the Emergency Preparedness Plan worked, each family member discussed their roles in the event of a crisis. Her father agreed to be a backup for their financial needs. Ben's mom was pleased to be a resource to provide care for the kids. Oliver said he'd take care of and feed all the animals. Ben's father volunteered to help with the animals, as well. Heather's mom traveled for her job but offered to help look after the children when she was in town.

Feeling supported and thankful, Heather slipped an arm around Ben.

After giving everyone time to ask questions, Heather handed each set of grandparents a PEP Binder, and handed the third copy to Oliver. "Oliver, we will keep the copy I gave you in your dad's office. I wanted you to have it for this meeting so you can become familiar with it."

After reviewing the PEP Binder, Ben took his mom, Heather's dad and Oliver to his office to review the Legacy Drawer.

Ben's dad and the twins went to the barn to see the horses. Heather and her mom headed to the kitchen to put the final touches on lunch. The weather was pleasant so they planned to eat on the back patio.

When the neighbor arrived for lunch, everyone found a seat around the picnic tables. Again, Heather expressed her gratitude and provided an overview of the PEP Plan for the neighbor. Each time Heather shared the plan with someone, she got excited, and she felt more confident about her family's future.

Heather answered her neighbor's questions and was pleased that he was willing to be a part of their PEP Plan. Heather made sure he knew the offer would be reciprocated. Heather said she'd be happy to help him with his PEP Plan when he was ready. Her neighbor liked the idea of being a reliable support for one another.

As Ben and Heather brought the meal and meeting to a close, they encouraged their loved ones to create their own PEP Plans. They gave everyone, including Oliver, a copy of the *Family Emergency Handbook*. Heather encouraged them to create their own plan and host their own training meeting and offered to be there for them.

By 3:00 PM, the kitchen was clean, and all the guests had gone home.

Ben smiled and pulled Heather into a half-hug. "Well, that went off without a hitch."

"And we got it done within sixty days. Now, I'm headed to the tub. I'll see you tomorrow!" Heather said with a laugh.

Monday, October 31st, 8:00 AM
Miles Corporation Headquarters

There was excitement in the air as Heather entered the boardroom. Mike, the CFO, was at his usual place at the head of the table and warmly greeted her as she took a seat.

Everyone else had already arrived and looked at Mike in appreciation.

It was the end of the 60-day challenge and every single manager had created a PEP Plan.

While they had originally done it for the bonus and time off, everyone agreed they had already received far greater benefits from doing the process.

Mike asked each person to share their experience with the team. When it was Heather's turn, she said, "I had no idea how complicated my life was until I created my PEP Plan. Everyone in my family chipped in to get it done, including the twins! When Oliver's grandparents, his mother's parents, heard about what we are doing, they offered to pay for our attorney so that it fit with the trust they had set up for Oliver after his mother passed away. Ben, Oliver and I signed our wills last week."

Heather continued, "My actual time to complete the process was one hour less than my estimated time. For me, it was helpful to know how much time to schedule. Completing this project has changed our family forever. I am extremely grateful to you and Mary for providing this opportunity."

As Heather was finishing, Mary, the CEO, took out a folder with a big smile on her face.

Mike said, "Now, I think Mary has something for you."

"Congratulations to you all for completing this challenge. You've earned your rewards." Mary handed everyone envelopes with bonus checks.

Monday, November 14th, 8:00 AM

Miles Corporation Headquarters

"Thanks to you," Mike said, "we have decided to roll out the Be Ready, Life Happens Training Program to the entire company. We are very excited to be able to provide this program to our team and couldn't have done it without you."

The managers around the table nodded and smiled.

Heather was happy to hear the company was willing to invest in the success of their team. A warm feeling of joy spread through her heart.

Mike said, "Heather suggested I share with you how we came up with this idea so that you can see the bigger picture." Heather was pleased Mike had remembered their conversation and valued her opinion. It felt so good to be part of a bigger mission. She hoped other forward-thinking companies would follow suit. Heather vowed to go the extra mile to make sure this rollout was successful.

After repeating the conversation he had had with Heather about bringing Conscious Capitalism and Legacy Planning together, Mike said, "Mary will provide an overview of the rollout. We still have a few details to nail down but didn't want to keep you waiting on our decision. You will receive a packet on Friday with all the information. For now, take note of the dates and times we will need your help."

All eyes moved to Mary, who explained, "The CPA believes rolling out the Be Ready, Life Happens Program will positively impact our profitability in several ways. He expects to see a reduction in presenteeism and absenteeism."

As she was speaking, Mike turned on his computer, which activated the giant screen with a PowerPoint slide.

We are facing an economic crisis at the family level that has global implications.

Mary continued, "We don't have the exact numbers, but we do know that some of our team members are providing unpaid help to their families. In caregiving terms, this assistance is called *informal caregiving*.

"According to Lisa Burden's July 22, 2019 article, 'The Economic Cost of Caregiving Could Double by 2050', the U.S. economy loses an estimated $25.2 billion per year from caregiver absenteeism. These numbers are expected to increase significantly as baby boomers age."

The next slide introduced the terms *absenteeism* and *presenteeism*. Mary explained, "Absenteeism is fairly easy to measure: missed time to leave early, arrive late, take the day off. Unfortunately, there is another and more costly productivity problem that is invisible and impossible to measure called *presenteeism*.

"According to Paul Hemp, author of the article 'Presenteeism: At Work – But Out of It', published in the October 2004 *Harvard Business Review* magazine, presenteeism happens when employees are at work, but not fully functioning.

"According to Hemp, 'In fact, presenteeism appears to be a much costlier problem than its productivity-reducing counterpart, absenteeism. And, unlike absenteeism, presenteeism isn't always apparent: You know when someone doesn't show up for work, but you often can't tell when—or how much—illness or a medical condition is hindering someone's performance.'"

Mary clasped her hands and looked around the table. "Many families struggle to survive, much less have the capicity to help someone else. But the truth is, we rarely deny a loved one's request for assistance, even when doing so jeopardizes our own livelihood. We believe this rollout will help all our team members, especially the ones who are informal caregivers."

Mary continued, "Our CPA anticipates the program will contribute to employee retention and lower the cost of employee turnover. Although it will take time to measure the impact of the program, we know what it will cost.

"While we aren't going to give everyone in the company a $1,000 bonus for creating a PEP Plan, we are providing resources to help them complete one. Based on your positive feedback we are moving forward with a company-wide program for team members to complete within 90 days."

As Mary stepped through the Power Point presentation on the big screen, she said, "We know that most of our team members don't have a will, so we are finalizing a contract with a new supplier of legal aid to supplement our benefits program. Team members will have the opportunity to sign up for legal aid services at the kickoff meeting on December 1st. We expect the legal aid fee to be less than $30 per team member, per month.

"For every team member that completes a PEP Plan by the end of February, we will reimburse their legal costs for the three months of the program. While I'd love 100% participation in the program, I'm realistic. Should a miracle occur, and all 250 team members participate, the cost would be less than $23,000. After considering all the additional costs, we feel like this is an excellent investment in our team. Now, Mike will fill you in on the details of the rollout plan."

All eyes returned to Mike, who said, "Please mark your calendars for the following dates: On Thursday, December 1st, Diane, Mary's Legacy Planner will be onsite to conduct a series of the Be Ready, Life Happens Workshops. Our training room can hold up to 60 people, so I've divided our team into five groups of fifty team members. We will be pulling people from various divisions so that we can keep the company running.

"Each team member will receive a copy of the *Family Emergency Handbook*. We want each of you to attend one session." Mike scheduled each manager, then continued, "Please be prepared to share your experience with your group. Don't sugarcoat your experience. Please be honest." Mike grinned wide as he looked around the room. "Let's make this roll-out a huge success!"

Professionally, Heather felt like she was on the ground floor of something big.

Thursday, November 24th, Thanksgiving Day
At Home on the Ranch

As the family gathered around the table to enjoy their traditional Thanksgiving meal, Heather was amazed at how quickly life had changed. The night in the barn and his mother's treasures had restored Oliver's good spirits.

It was comforting to know that when, not if, a crisis occurred, their closest friends and family were prepared to step in and help. As an added bonus, three sets of grandparents were working on their own PEP Plans and had promised to get it done by the end of the year. Heather and Ben were closer. Best of all, they felt totally confident that no matter what life threw at them, their family would thrive.

Find Your *Why*

When we don't have a strong *Why*, making a change can be challenging. Brain biases can get in the way of our success. In the Frye family short story, Heather's *Why* was a day off and a $1,000 bonus.

What's your *Why*? If you already know your compelling motivation to complete a PEP plan, write it in the space below. But, if you could use some help, use the "Five *Why* Exercise" below to identify your motivating *Why*.

You may find your *Why* before the fifth *Why*, as I did in the example below. If you need more than five *Whys*, keep going. You will know when you have found your motivating *Why* when you move from your head to your heart. Then, you can stop

Here is an example of how I used the Five *Why* Exercise to find my *Why*.

1. I want to create a PEP Plan because <u>I want to make it easier for my children to help me</u>.

2. I want to <u>make it easier for my children to help me</u> because <u>I don't want to be a burden to them</u>.

3. <u>I don't want to be a burden to them</u> because <u>I love them</u>. I will create a PEP Plan because I love my children and want to make it easier for them to help me, so I won't be a burden to them.

Five *Why* Exercise

1. I want to create a PEP Plan because (1st *Why* _____).
2. I want to (1st *Why* _____) because (2nd *Why* _____).
3. I want to (2nd *Why* _____) because (3rd *Why* _____).
4. I want to (3rd *Why* _____) because (4th *Why* _____).
5. I want to (4th *Why* _____) because (5th *Why* _____).

> **Use your motivating *Why* to stay motivated, on track and outsmart your brain!**

Commitment Contract

Good intentions aren't enough.

Too often we find ourselves on the road to . . . well, you know where.

Identifying a heartfelt *Why* is a good start. Making a commitment to yourself is an additional step to help you outsmart your brain.

In the spaces below, write your name on each blank line, then sign and date the contract.

I, _____, believe in the principle: **Be Ready. Life Happens.** And I commit to completing the steps in this process.

I, _____, am willing to be uncomfortable. I commit to courageous action to do what it takes to create a PEP Plan.

I, _____, further understand that this process may have some ups and downs, and I commit to taking small baby steps to build momentum and complete this process.

I, _____, will remember my *Why* to stay motivated and use it to outsmart my brain.

_____

(Signature)

_____

(Date)

"The journey of a thousand miles begins with a single step."

— **Lao Tzu**

Step One: Organize Your Legacy Drawer

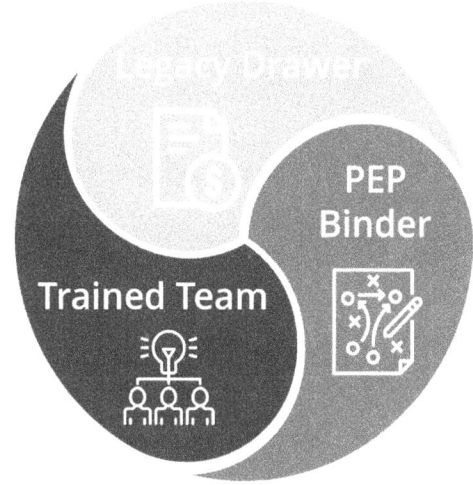

To complete this step, you will organize your important documents into the following twelve sections.

Section 1: Medical Information

Section 2: Home

Section 3: Loved Ones

Section 4: Legal Documents

Section 5: Subscriptions and Security

Section 6: Bank Accounts and Credit Cards

Section 7: Assets

Section 8: Liabilities

Section 9: Insurance

Section 10: Personal Information

Section 11: End-of-Life Plan

Section 12: Communication Lists

Section 1: Medical Information

The purpose of this section is to make it easy to quickly provide accurate medical information. In a medical emergency, having this information readily available could mean the difference between life and death.

Providing accurate and up to date health information protects your health and eliminates UNNECESSARY STRESS for your family.

> When my husband, Gerald, was diagnosed with cancer, we suddenly found ourselves in a new world of ongoing doctor visits.
>
> In September, on his 71st birthday, Gerald had surgery to install a port so he could start chemo treatments. These were scheduled every two weeks, and he had a lab visit before each treatment. Each time, the doctors wanted to know his current medication list and medical history.
>
> His current medical condition was changing on a weekly basis. As a problem-solver, I created the forms in this section to make it easier to communicate Gerald's quickly changing medical condition. He used a three-ring binder to make it easy to carry his information with him.
>
> It was an empowering step to take during a challenging time.
>
> Gerald finished twelve rounds of chemo on March 2, 2020, days before the world shut down for the COVID-19 pandemic.
>
> It's been almost three years since Gerald's diagnosis, and he continues to thrive. I tease him about being an overachiever because less than 10 people per million get appendix cancer, and he has remained healthy during a global pandemic.
>
> Designing and living your significant life is an important aspect of the legacy planning process. It has been instrumental in really enjoying life while living with cancer.

The Medical section is one of the meatiest sections of your PEP Plan. There are a total of seven possible forms to create for each person in your family. If you are caring for aging adults or dependent children, complete medical forms for them as well.

You may not need all the forms in this section. Complete the ones that pertain to each family member's unique medical situation.

Family Medical History

When doctors have access to family medical history, they can identify patterns of disease within the family to provide better care to their patients.

For a typical non-blended family, you will complete three family medical history forms. One for you. One for your partner. One for your children. There is a sample Family Medical History form in the Appendix for your use.

If you have children from a previous marriage or adopted children and have access to their family medical history, complete a separate form for them. If you don't have children, then you'll fill out two forms for you and your partner. If you're single, do it for yourself.

If your ancestors are gone and you don't have their medical history, fill out what you can and move on. Later, if it is a priority, you can interview older relatives who might know your ancestor's medical history or find death certificates. Ancestry.com is an excellent resource.

Personal Medical History: Document your personal medical history. Be sure to capture your vision and dental history as well.

What is your blood type?

Do you donate blood on a regular basis?

What blood bank do you use?

Have you ever had surgery? What kind? When?

What diagnoses have you received?

Do you have any dietary restrictions?

Do you have any allergies? How do you react? What treatment is required?

Do you use wearables: a mouth guard, hearing aids, glasses or contacts?

Do you use a c-pap machine or other medical device?

Create a record of vaccines for the flu, pneumonia, shingles, COVID, etc. Notate the manufacturer and date received for COVID vaccinations. Include vaccine shot history for children.

Current Medical Condition: Now that you've completed your medical history, transfer your ongoing medical conditions here. Make sure you include your blood type, allergies and their treatment, and wearables.

Current Medications and Supplements: Create a list of your current medications. Be sure to include the prescribing physician and dosage. Are you taking over-the-counter medications? Eyedrops? Topical ointments? Include them on this list.

Current Medical Equipment and Supplies: If you don't use any medical equipment or supplies, please count your blessings and skip this list. Create a list of current Medical Equipment and Supplies to track equipment that is owned vs. rented. For leased equipment include the contact information to return the equipment.

Current Health Insurance and Veteran's Benefits: For me, making a copy of both sides of my insurance card was the quickest way to capture this information. If you prefer, make a list of your current health insurance and any veteran's benefits you receive.

Medical Contact List: Create a contact list of your current doctors. Include their name, specialty, address and phone number. If you use a portal to access information, include the web address, your username and password. Each doctor may have their own portal. Capture all of them.

Medical Activities Checklist

Complete medical forms for everyone in your household. Use the checklist to calculate how many forms you will need to complete.

- ☐ **Create a Family Medical History of your ancestors.** Place one copy in the Medical section of your Legacy Drawer. Place the second copy in the PEP Binder behind the Medical tab.

- ☐ **Create a Personal Medical History.** Place one copy in the Medical section of your Legacy Drawer. Place the second copy in the PEP Binder behind the Medical tab.

- ☐ **Create a Current Medical Condition.** Place one copy in the Medical section of your Legacy Drawer. Place the second copy in the PEP Binder behind the Medical tab.

- ☐ **Create a Current Medical Equipment and Supplies List.** Place one copy in the Medical section of your Legacy Drawer. Place the second copy in the PEP Binder behind the Medical tab.

- ☐ **Create a Current Health Insurance and Veteran's Benefits List.** Place one copy in the Medical section of your Legacy Drawer. Place the second copy in the PEP Binder behind the Medical tab.

- ☐ **Create a Medical Contact List.** Place one copy in the Medical section of your Legacy Drawer. Place the second copy in the PEP Binder behind the Medical tab.

- ☐ **Locate permanent health records and file them in this section.**

Section 2: Home

The purpose of this section is to make it easy for your PEP Team to protect your home in your absence. You will create a contact list and guest instructions for each residential property you own and set up files for your permanent records.

> Not every situation is an emergency. We wrote our first guest instructions for pet sitters when we lived on a 30-acre ranch in Boerne, TX. My friends lobbied for the opportunity to stay at the ranch while we were gone. We had 2 horses, 2 donkeys, 4 cats and a dog. In exchange for taking care of the animals, our friends had an opportunity to enjoy the spectacular Texas Hill Country views from the back porch.

There are two forms to complete for this section, plus an optional bonus form, the Home Maintenance Checklist.

Home Contact List

Make a list that includes helpful neighbors, repair service providers, utility companies, maintenance contractors, property managers, preferred real estate agents, homeowner associations, etc. Create a separate list for each of your residential properties. It's faster to find information when it's organized by location.

Guest Instructions

If you've ever stayed in a vacation home, you've seen a guest instruction sheet. It provides important information for an enjoyable and safe stay and includes information to access the internet, security codes, a description of amenities, the location of supplies, as well as emergency contact information.

See the sample Guest Instructions form in the Appendix to write a guest instruction sheet for each residential property you own. Include a calendar of weekly events such as lawn mowing, trash pickup or pool cleaning services. Be sure to start with any safety information. We've owned two small ranches in Texas, so our Safety-First section includes poisonous snakes, insects, skunks and porcupines.

Create a quick draft then ask someone you know to review the information and provide feedback.

To help you get started, I've provided a sample of our guest instructions in the Appendix.

Home Files

File title policies, deeds, warranties and other permanent documents in the Home section of your Legacy Drawer.

Home Maintenance Checklist (Optional)

Being married to a retired mechanical engineer has many perks. Over the past 25 years, Gerald has kept our homes perfectly maintained without the aid of a home maintenance checklist. For the rest of us who don't have his skills, the Home Maintenance Checklist provides a tool for maintaining and protecting one of our biggest investments. This is a helpful document, not a critical one. Create your own checklist from the sample in the Appendix.

If you already have a good home maintenance checklist, skip this form.

Home Checklist

- ☐ **Create 2 Home Contact Lists.** Place one copy in the Home section of the Legacy Drawer. Place the second copy in the PEP Binder behind the Home tab.

- ☐ **Create 2 copies of the Guest Instructions.** Place one copy in the Home section of the Legacy Drawer. Place the second copy in the PEP Binder behind the Home tab.

- ☐ **Locate important documents and file them in the Home Section of your Legacy Drawer.**

- ☐ **Optional: Complete two copies of the Home Maintenance Checklist in the Appendix.** Place one copy in the Home section of the Legacy Drawer. Place the second copy in the PEP Binder behind the Home tab.

Section 3: Loved Ones

If you don't have minor children or dependent adults, household pets or farm animals, you can skip this section and move on to the next section.

> My daughter and her husband have three children under the age of nine. At least once a year they schedule an adult only trip to reconnect and recharge. While they are gone, an army of friends and family step in to take care of their children, dogs, hermit crabs, bearded dragon and fish. The systems they have in place to go on vacation can also be implemented in an emergency.

Many families provide care to dependent adult children and/or aging adults and aren't comfortable getting away to rest and relax. Self-care is a critical component of successful caregiving. Not only does a PEP Plan help in an emergency, it provides confidence for caregivers to take a much-needed break. It is important to empower your PEP Team to provide care for your loved ones in your absence with legal documents such as a Power of Attorney (POA).

The pet forms in this section were created for our pet sitter when we traveled. Now they are part of our PEP Plan.

The purpose of this section is to create documents that make it easier for your PEP Team to ensure the safety of your loved ones, which include minor children, dependent adults, pets and farm animals.

Caring for Dependents (Minor Children and Dependent Adults)

The level of detail you need to include in this section will vary by your dependent's ability to communicate and care for themselves. The greater their ability to communicate their needs and take care of themselves, the less you will need to document.

I've always found it easier to edit a document than it is to create one from scratch, so I have included several sample forms for this section in the Appendix. Adopt them as necessary to create a document that works for your situation.

Please consult an attorney to review any documents you create to meet your state's requirements and ensure they are adequate for your needs.

Ultimately, you want to document the critical information to provide care for each dependent to ensure their safety and normalize their life in your absence or during emergencies. Include pertinent legal documents, medical records and care forms.

Animal Files

Create a separate pet form for each pet.

Create a consent for care form for your pets, either combined, or separately.

If you have farm animals, review the two forms in the Appendix and pick the one that suits your needs.

The **Farm Animal** Record works well for animals that you have named, such as horses and pet pigs.

The **Herd** Record works well for animals that are more investment than pets, such as horses, cattle, sheep or other herd animals. Most breeders have a quality record-keeping system. The Herd Record protects your investment by providing care instructions, contact information for helpful neighbors, the veterinarian, emergency veterinarian, vaccination records, the farrier and other service providers.

File registration papers and other permanent important documents in this section of your Legacy Drawer.

Loved Ones Activities Checklist

- ☐ **Create a Caregiving Plan for Dependents** for each minor child or dependent adult living in your home. Place one copy in Loved Ones section of your Legacy Drawer. Place the second copy in the PEP Binder behind the Loved Ones tab.

- ☐ **Create a Consent to Treat Dependents** form for each minor child or dependent adult living in your home. Place one copy in Loved Ones section of your Legacy Drawer. Place the second copy in the PEP Binder behind the Loved Ones tab.

- ☐ **Create two copies of the appropriate record (Pet, Farm or Herd).** Place one copy in the Loved Ones Section of your Legacy Drawer. Place the second copy in the PEP Binder behind the Loved Ones tab.

- ☐ **Create a POA for Pet Emergency Care** form for your pets. Place one copy in Loved Ones section of your Legacy Drawer. Place the second copy in the PEP Binder behind the Loved Ones tab.

- ☐ **Create a POA for Farm Animal Emergency Care** form for your farm animals. Place one copy in Loved Ones section of your Legacy Drawer. Place the second copy in the PEP Binder behind the Loved Ones tab.

- ☐ **Locate important documents and file them in the Loved Ones Section.**

Section 4: Legal Documents

Just in case you skipped the disclaimer at the front of the book, I'm repeating myself here, because it is important that you know: this book **does not provide legal advice**. Please, contact your professional advisors for legal advice.

Let's get on the same page concerning the term *will*. A *will* serves dual purposes. It protects you while you are alive and tidies up your life after you die. I will use *will*, *estate plan* and *legal documents* interchangeably.

They all refer to a group of essential estate planning documents that, at a minimum, contain the following:

- Last Will and Testament
- Statutory Power of Attorney
- Power of Attorney for Health Care
- DNR-Do Not Resuscitate

This is a very basic list. Most quality estate plans include additional documents. Talk to your estate planning professional about your needs.

Each state is different, so if you move from one state to another, you need a new *will*.

Did you know that spouses can't make legal decisions for each other without legal authority? If either you or your spouse doesn't have a *will* yet, you aren't authorized to help each other.

Few people recognize that the best time to get their first set of legal documents is on their 18th birthday. The first set may only include the documents that protect you while you are alive because most 18-year-old adults don't have a lot of assets.

It sounds bizarre, but providing a *will* as a birthday gift for newly adult children sets a positive example for the rest of their life. It's also a great time to discuss how you can support them in designing and living their best life by using their gifts and talents to make the world a better place.

> **Nancy's story**
>
> Nancy was a financial advisor working for a prestigious firm, and she wanted to learn more about Legacy Planning.
>
> During our meeting I asked her my three-foot question: *Do you have an updated will or estate plan?* She admitted that although she had a young daughter, neither Nancy nor her husband had a will. We talked about the importance of having a will, especially with a minor child.
>
> A few months later, I followed up with her to see how she was doing. Between our two calls, tragedy had struck her family. Unfortunately, her husband had died from COVID. They had not obtained their wills before his untimely death.
>
> Here's the greater tragedy: Nancy ended up in a custody battle with her in-laws. It was an unfounded attempt by her husband's parents to gain custody. Thank goodness the court ruled in Nancy's favor.
>
> The stress of losing her husband was unavoidable. The stress of being sued for custody of her daughter was UNNECESSARY STRESS that could have been avoided.
>
> It didn't have to be this way.
>
> This is another example of intending to do something *someday*. The day after the crisis is much too late. There aren't any do overs when it comes to death.

There is a nuance to this story.

Until Nancy experienced the consequences of being unprepared, she was ambivalent about helping her clients prepare. Professionally, she hadn't been trained to lead clients through this uncomfortable conversation, and until her experience, she wasn't comfortable talking about death.

After her ordeal, Nancy became a better advisor. She has her will and *insists* her clients get their legal affairs in order.

If you already have an updated will, congratulations!

If you don't have an updated will, choose a date to obtain one, preferably within 30 days. And commit to getting it done.

Legal Documents Activities Checklist

☐ **Move legal documents to the Legal Document section of your Legacy Drawer.** Write a note that includes the contact information for your Executor, Backup Executor and attorney and place it on top of the file.

If you don't have a *will* or estate plan yet, complete the steps below. Remember everyone over the age of 18 needs legal documents.

1. Commit to a date for getting your *will* done. (I suggest 30 days or less.)

2. Decide on your budget. I hear ALL THE TIME: "I have no budget!" Yes, you do, whether you have the courage to acknowledge it, or not. When you die without a will, the state will settle your affairs. There are EXTRA and AVOIDABLE costs for dying without a will. These are set by your state and are non-negotiable. The *harsh truth* is this isn't a matter of a budget. It's a matter of priority. It's time to outsmart your brain. Get creative. Is there a parent or grandparent who would gift you a will as a Christmas gift or early birthday gift?

3. Find your *whos*. Ask for referrals from people you know and trust. As a last resort, there are several online companies that offer inexpensive services. One challenge with these services is that each state has different laws that the online services may miss. Opting for cheaper may cost you more in the long run if you end up with documents that aren't legal in your state.

4. To help you prepare for your first meeting with your planning professional, refer to the Preparing for the Will Conversation in the Appendix.

Section 5: Subscriptions and Security

Congratulations for making it this far! The good news is, it gets easier from here. You will continue to organize documents and create forms, but they will stay in your Legacy Drawer. You do not need to include them in your PEP Binder.

The purpose of this section is to organize your subscriptions, offsite facilities, and passwords to make it easy for your PEP Team to protect your credit and manage your offsite storage locations.

It used to be easier to track and pay bills because they showed up in your mailbox. Now, we can receive bills through a phone app, by text and email. We can set up autopayments on our credit card or request a direct withdrawal from our bank account. I am still in awe that I can purchase movies and sign up for new services from my TV! Because there are so many ways to get billed for subscriptions and memberships, it can be difficult to keep up.

For this section, you will create a Subscriptions List, Storage and Security List for offsite storage and instructions for locating passwords.

Subscriptions List: Create a list of your current subscriptions. Examples include: club memberships, toll tag, airline miles, magazine/newspapers, licensed software, mobile phone carriers, entertainment apps such as Netflix, Hulu and Disney+, donations to church and nonprofit organizations. Include how you receive your bill notification, contact information and any login information to access your account. For example, when my toll tag balance gets low, my credit card is automatically charged $40.00. When possible, include a renewal date, but don't let this bit of information slow you down. It is nice to know, not essential. Gather information about your subscriptions and autopayments. If needed, review your credit card statements and bank statements for charges. If you have a bill set up for autopay, treat it as if it is a subscription even if it technically isn't one. For example, my long-term insurance, health, life, auto and umbrella insurance policies are all set up for automatic payment. Some are billed monthly, others are billed every six months, and one is set up for annual payment. For payments like these, be sure to include the date, or approximate date, the charge will occur.

Storage and Security List: Between safety deposit boxes, mailbox centers and self-storage units, we can end up with a handful of keys. Label each of the keys. Create a list of offsite facilities and location of keys. Be sure to include any necessary access information like lock combinations, key codes, renewal dates, usernames or passwords. This section is also where you can list the places you store hard drive media and digital assets, as well as online media, such as Apple Cloud, Amazon Drive, Dropbox, MediaFire, and Microsoft OneDrive. Who can serve as your online media agent? You will want to prepare them in advance to successfully serve in this role.

Passwords: How many times have you hit the reset password because you couldn't remember your password? If you are like I was before I got organized, at least once a week! If your family needs to reset a password for you, they will need access to your phone and/or computer. Make a list of your equipment, where you normally store it and the login information to your equipment. How are you currently keeping your passwords? My husband used to keep a handwritten list of his passwords, but it got overwhelming. We recently upgraded to a software solution that generated a "key." We filed the key in this section of our Legacy Drawer. Do what works for you and use this section to store critical information.

Subscriptions and Security Activities Checklist

- ☐ **Create a Subscriptions List for your subscriptions.** File it in the Subscriptions and Security section of your Legacy Drawer.

- ☐ **Create a Storage and Security List for your offsite storage units and online or hard drive media storage. Be sure to include the location of your keys.** File it in the Subscriptions and Security section of your Legacy Drawer.

- ☐ **Create a Passwords List for your passwords.** File it in the Subscriptions and Security section of your Legacy Drawer.

Section 6: Bank Accounts and Credit Cards

The purpose of this section is to organize your bank account and credit card information to make it easy for your PEP Team to protect your credit and avoid lost assets.

Bank Accounts

Make a list of your bank accounts. Include the bank name (or credit union), location, account information and how you access your account. Be sure to add the website, username and password for accessing your accounts.

If you have a personal relationship with your banker, include their contact information.

Credit Cards

My husband and I have three credit cards each. I completed this section in ten minutes that resulted in two pieces of paper for each of us.

I made a copy of my three credit cards (front and back) and a copy of Gerald's three credit cards (front and back). The contact information is already on the cards, and I wrote the website, user name and password on the bottom of the page.

For this section, create a Bank Accounts List, copy your credit cards and set up files to store permanent records.

Bank Accounts and Credit Cards Activities Checklist

- ☐ **Create a Bank Accounts List for your bank accounts.** File it in the Bank Accounts and Credit Cards section of your Legacy Drawer.
- ☐ **Create a Credit Cards file for your credit cards.** File it behind the Bank Accounts and Credit Cards tab of your Legacy Drawer.

Section 7: Assets

The purpose of this section is to organize your assets to make it easy for your PEP Team to protect your assets and credit.

Financial Assets: Use your balance sheet or create a list of assets as your guide. While financial assets are typically defined as cash, stocks and bonds, if you have other assets listed on your balance sheet, include them here. Many clients consider retirement accounts and accounts receivables as financial assets.

If you have questions about your balance sheet, contact your CPA. Create one file per asset and include permanent account documents in the file. To keep your Legacy Drawer files of manageable size, store periodic reports in your current tax-year files.

When you move, it's easy to lose track of assets like utility deposits, insurance refunds, and store credits. I've included a resource in the Appendix, Unclaimed Assets, to help you find potential lost assets for you and your loved ones. Check every state that you've lived in.

Real Estate Files: My real estate files are so big, they take up an entire drawer in a fire-proof filing cabinet. As a second-generation manager of investment properties, I inherited thick files that had thirty years of information. Some of our documents are so old, they were typed on onion skin paper. If your real estate files will fit into your Legacy Drawer, move them there to make it easier to find them. File important documents in this file.

Property Contact List: Remember the Home Contact List you created for your home(s)? You will do the same for each investment property you own. Create a Property Contact List that includes your tenant, repair service providers, utility providers, maintenance contractors, real estate agents, property managers, taxing authorities and insurance agents. Make it easy to protect your investment real estate by creating a Property Contact List. Creating a contact list by location makes it easier to find information in a hurry.

Other Assets: The list of other assets is too extensive to list each possible item in this book. Examples include: trademarks, precious metals, Bitcoin, internal loans, artwork, royalties, farm animals, antique automobiles, collectables, utility deposits, etc. Create a file for these assets. Include an estimate of value and a suggestion for their disposition. Protecting your Bitcoin accounts requires additional diligence. For example, when a Bitcoin investor died, the key to his Bitcoin account was never located and all those assets vanished. I've heard horror stories of lost Bitcoin accounts that were stored on computers that were lost or destroyed.

Assets Activities Checklist

- ☐ **Print a balance sheet or create a list of assets. Review the list.** Are there any assets not listed? If so, make corrections.

- ☐ **Set up a separate file for each asset in the Assets section of your Legacy Drawer.** Organize files in the order that they are listed on your balance sheet or list.

- ☐ **Create a Property Contact List for each investment property you own.**

Section 8: Liabilities

The purpose of this section is to organize your liabilities to make it easy for your PEP Team to protect your credit.

If you are debt free you can skip this section! Being debt free is an accomplishment to celebrate. Congratulations!

If not, use your balance sheet or make a list of your loans and credit card debt to organize your liabilities.

As you did for the assets, organize liabilities in the same order as your balance sheet/list, and organize your files in the order that they appear on your balance sheet/list.

Ideally, you already have files set up for your liabilities, and it's only a matter of reorganizing existing files. If not, organizing this section of your Legacy Drawer will take longer. And that's OK. The time you are investing now will save time later.

In this section you will use your balance sheet or liabilities list as a guide for setting up your files for mortgages, loans, escrow accounts and other liabilities. Be sure to document internal loans, such as a private loan from family members, friends or loans made between your own entities.

Liabilities Activities Checklist

- ☐ **Print a balance sheet or create a list.** Review the list. Are there any liabilities not listed? If so, correct your balance sheet or list.

- ☐ **Set up a separate file for each liability** in the Liabilities section of your Legacy Drawer. Organize files in the order that they are listed on your balance sheet or list.

Section 9: Insurance

The purpose of this section is to make it easy to locate your insurance information. Create an Insurance Contact List and set up files for your permanent records.

The Insurance section is very straightforward when you know where your current policy information is located. Include all types of insurance in this section, including, but not limited to, health, life, medical, property, umbrella, long-term care, business, jewelry, etc. Use your policies to locate the address, expiration date, and premium payments. Identify someone to serve as an advocate with your insurance companies. Now would be a good time to double check the beneficiaries on any life insurance policies.

It will be more challenging if you can't find your documents. Call your agent and/or insurance company. Ask them for your policy information and request a copy of your policy.

If your agent sends you a digital copy of your policy, copy it to a jump drive to file in your Legacy Drawer, or store it on your computer in a digital legacy drawer. However you file it, make sure your PEP Team can locate the policies.

Insurance Activities Checklist

- ☐ **Create an Insurance Contact List for all insurance policies.** Be sure to include the policy number and expiration date. File it in the Insurance section of your Legacy Drawer.

- ☐ **File certificates of insurance, proof of insurance and policies in this section of your Legacy Drawer.** Remember, this file is not to be used for bills or statements.

Section 10: Personal Information

The purpose of this section is to make it easy for your team to find your personal information.

> When my dad's sister, Becky, passed away, I received a call from her granddaughter. She was at the funeral home with her aunt and uncles, trying to answer questions to obtain a death certificate. No one could remember Becky's mother's real name. They only knew her as Granny.
>
> They called me because they knew I had obtained a death certificate for my father years before. Had they not been wracked with grief, they probably would've remembered Granny's name was Ruthia Lou. It's hard to think straight when you are in pain.
>
> When we are proactive, and complete our own Vital Statistics form, we are saving our loved ones from PREVENTABLE STRESS.

Vital Statistics

Until you have experienced filling out a death certificate, you don't know what you will need. After my clients get past the uncomfortableness of facing their own mortality, they complete the Vital Statistics form in minutes. Complete the form in the Appendix as a gift for your family.

File Important Documents

Create a separate file or envelope for each family member. The personal section is the best place to organize permanent personal information such as driver's license, birth certificate, marriage license, divorce paperwork, social security card and passport. Include personal information that you deem important, such as college transcripts or diplomas. In my file, I've even included a few of my favorite poems that I've written.

Personal Information Activities Checklist

- ☐ **Create a Vital Statistics form.** This form contains the information to obtain a death certificate. Place one copy in the Personal section of your Legacy Drawer.

- ☐ **Locate personal information and file it in this section.**

Section 11: End-of-Life Plan

The purpose of this section is to communicate your end-of-life decisions to empower your PEP Team with confidence to honor your last wishes. For many clients, this is the most emotionally challenging section to complete.

> **Christy's Story**
>
> Christy brought her father to a workshop about a year before her mom passed. As her primary caregiver, Christy used the tools she'd learned in the workshop to initiate conversations about death with her mom. She wanted to understand her mom's end-of-life decisions.
>
> Her mom had heart issues and made two trips to the hospital by ambulance in three months. At 37, Christy found herself alone in the emergency room with a request to sign a Do Not Resuscitate (DNR) form for her mom. One sister was at work, and the other lived hours away. Her dad was out of town.
>
> Later, when Christy called to thank me for the workshop, she shared her experience. When faced with signing the DNR, her initial thought was, "I can't make this decision for my mom."
>
> Then Christy remembered the conversations she had with her mom. She knew exactly what her mom wanted. Christy realized, *I'm not the one making the decision. I'm honoring the decision Mom already made. Mom is counting on me to do the right thing for her.*
>
> So, despite the difficulty of the situation, sitting alone in the emergency room, Christy signed the DNR.
>
> Afterward, despite the crushing sadness, Christy felt a bit of peace. There was no guesswork. *She* had been the one her mom could count on. And because of that, Christy could focus on grieving the loss of her beloved mother.
>
> During our phone call, Christy said, "The end-of-life conversations I had with mom saved me a lifetime of guilt and therapy." Even during the saddest times of your life, you can experience a heartbeat of peace that comes from being prepared.

Memento mori is the Latin phrase that means "remember that you must die."

It becomes much easier to complete the end-of-life plan when you embrace *memento mori*.

For this section, complete the final instructions form, write a draft obituary, create a Pre-Arrangement Contact List, and set up files for your permanent records.

Final Instructions

Empower your family to honor your wishes by providing them with needed information. Give yourself time to review this form to make decisions about your body and your celebration of life after you pass. Make it easy for your family by communicating your wishes.

Most clients are able to complete this section in two half-hour sessions. Start by reading and reflecting on the available choices concerning the disposition of your body and celebration of your life. Be courageous. Give yourself time to reflect, but don't wait for *someday* to complete it.

After a few days, complete the form with your current choices. You can always go back and make changes. Once you are done, place your Advanced Planning and Final Instructions form in your Legacy Drawer.

Draft Obituary

> Toastmasters International is an excellent organization to improve your leadership and speaking skills. When we moved to Boerne, TX our club meetings were held at an assisted living center.
>
> Don was in his late eighties and a resident. He had been a Toastmaster for over six decades. His "draft obituary" speech was so riveting, powerful and inspirational that I decided to write my own draft obituary.
>
> Then, I sent it to my children on New Year's Eve without providing any context. Needless to say, I received some phone calls the next day from worried family members inquiring about my health. It took several calls to reassure them I was fine and simply aiming to prevent future stress for them.

Writing a draft obituary is a powerful exercise. Not only does it reduce UNNECESSARY STRESS for your family by providing factual information, it can also help you design and live your best life. When you consider how you want to be remembered, your legacy, you realize you still have time to accomplish big dreams. You have time to build better relationships with the people you love. You have time to avoid common end-of-life regrets. Here's the magic: you can include your dreams in your draft obituary. If it doesn't make it to your obituary, it isn't important. You design your significant life by identifying what you want included in your draft obituary and spend your remaining time on earth to live up to being that person. Update your draft when your aspirations change.

Use the prompts in the Appendix to write your draft obituary. It provides amazing clarity about what's truly important in life.

- Set your intention to complete this form in two half-hour sessions.
- Use the first session to quickly answer the writing prompts.
- Use the second session to edit your first draft.
- Print a copy of you draft obituary and file it in your Legacy Drawer.

Pre-Arrangement Contact List

Gerald and I purchased prepaid cremation services. It even includes a "travel policy" in case we die away from home. Make it easy to find information about pre-need investments by creating a contact list with account or policy numbers.

If you have proof of payment, file it in this section of your Legacy Drawer.

End-of-Life Plan Activities Checklist

- ☐ **Complete the Final Instructions** form. Empower your family to honor your wishes by providing them with needed information. Give yourself time to review this form to make decisions about your body and your celebration of life after you pass. Place one copy in the End-of-Life Plan section of your Legacy Drawer.

- ☐ **Write a draft obituary.** Place one copy in the End-of-Life Plan section of your Legacy Drawer.

- ☐ **Create a Pre-Arrangement Contact List.** Place one copy in the End-of-Life Plan section of your Legacy Drawer.

Section 12: Communication Lists

The purpose of this section is to make it easy to locate contact information to communicate with family, friends, professional advisors, and business partners.

The Emergency Contact List includes the contact information for your designated agents named in legal documents and your professional advisors. You have already created contact lists to protect your health, wealth and loved ones, so you don't need to list them again here. Think about your life. Outside of the groups mentioned, is there someone you need to add to this list? Are you an officer of an organization? Do you regularly donate time to a nonprofit organization? Include their contact information on this list if you want them to be contacted in case of an emergency. If you own your own business, do you have a succession plan? If not, it would be a good idea to create one after you complete your PEP Plan. For now, who is your emergency contact? Include them on this list.

The Personal Contact List includes your family members and personal friends. If you have a Christmas or holiday card list, you already have a jump-start! If you don't have a list yet, but always wanted to get organized, this is your opportunity!

Notification of Death Contact List includes everyone on your emergency appointment list, as well as your extended family members, close friends and business connections.

Do you feel the need to create a DO NOT CONTACT LIST? This is a list of people you wouldn't want contacted. This is a difficult topic, but the truth is, some people make this choice.

Here is a word of caution: the person you don't want contacted will eventually find out. Asking family members to keep a secret about an emergency or death puts them in an awkward situation, especially when they have a relationship with the estranged family member/friend.

From experience, I've found DO NOT CONTACT lists don't work. Word spreads, especially when there has been a tragedy.

As a Certified Legacy Planning Advisor™, I've facilitated difficult conversations between family members who need an outsider to lead the conversation. While my goal is to build communication and trust within the family, reconciliation can only happen when both parties want to heal the relationship.

Ironically, it's the person who refuses to reconcile who typically makes the DO NOT CONTACT List.

For this section, you will create an Emergency Contact List, Personal Contact List and Notification of Death Contact List and file them in your Legacy Drawer.

Communication Lists Activities Checklist

- ☐ **Create an Emergency Contact List.** File it in the Communication section of your Legacy Drawer.

- ☐ **Create a Personal Contact List.** File it in the Communication section of your Legacy Drawer.

- ☐ **Create a Notification of Death Contact List.** File it in the Communication section of your Legacy Drawer.

Step Two: Create Your PEP Binder

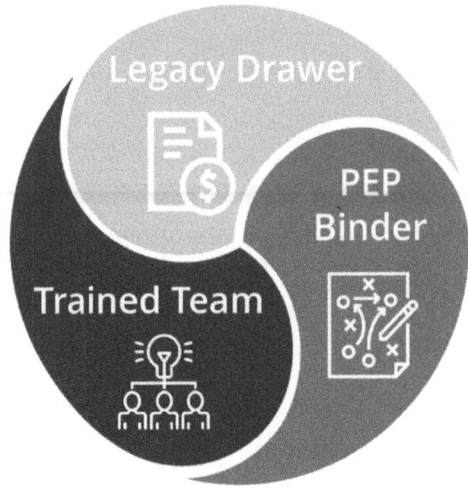

Ta da! You have already created your PEP Binder!

You were instructed to file an extra copy of the forms you completed in the first three sections in your binder. The rest of your Legacy Drawer contains sensitive information that doesn't need to be included in your binder.

The binder is your PEP Binder. It is the foundation for a training manual to train your PEP Team so they can confidently assist you during an unexpected crisis.

You have two extra tabs to include additional helpful information. Some clients add their communication lists, others include their medical power of attorney and other legal documents.

This is your PEP Binder, customize it to your needs.

Your PEP Binder is a valuable resource. You now have a portable file that is easily duplicated to protect your health, wealth and loved ones. It contains critical information in one place to assist your PEP Team to handle your affairs in case you become incapacitated.

Now that you have organized your Legacy Drawer and created your PEP Binder, you are ready to train your team.

Even if you haven't finished your estate planning, it's time to identify who will be on your PEP Team and begin the training process.

Step Three: Train Your Team

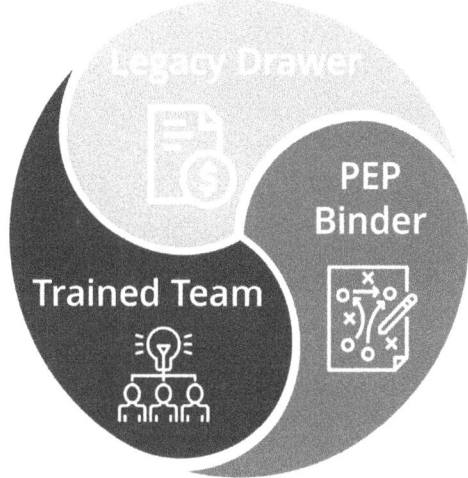

When my daughters became informal caregivers for their dad, they divided their duties. One daughter became his health care advocate and the other became the point of contact for his insurance company. They delegated care of his cows to the neighbor and worked together to keep his company and finances in order.

All of this was done without training. They fell into their roles using their natural gifts and talents. Everything got done, but it wasn't easy.

Over and over, I see families suffer from failing to plan before the crisis begins.

It is especially hard for an older widow whose husband has died, when he was the one who handled the finances. In his absence, the widow's grief is compounded by the added terror of managing her finances for the first time.

With your Legacy Drawer and PEP Binder done, identify the people who are most likely to help in an emergency. These are your PEP Team Leaders, the ones you can train to assist you.

I realize this is a radical idea, but doesn't it make sense?

Your life circumstances will determine who needs to be on your team. Use the questions below to identify who to ask to be on your team.

> Do you have trusted advisors who can help? Do you own your own company? Do you have a partnership?
>
> Do you have dependent children who need care? Do you have adult children who can help you? Are you married? Do you have aging parents who are relying on your help?
>
> Do you have pets? Farm animals?
>
> Do you have a home, or multiple homes?
>
> Do you have the financial resources to thrive during an emergency?

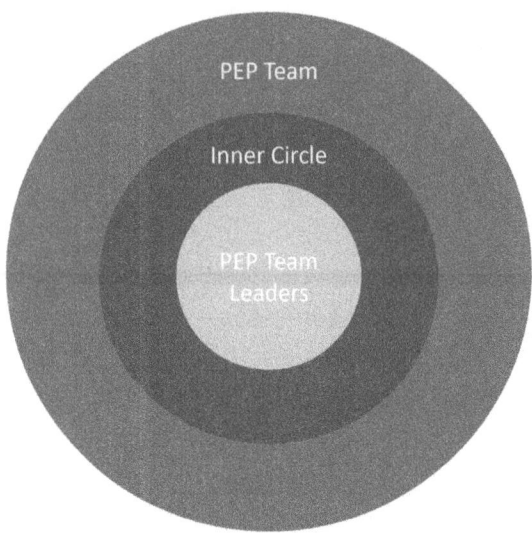

Start with your inner circle. These are the people you are consciously, or unconsciously, counting on to assist you when you need help. Who is willing and able to help? Make a list of the friends, family and neighbors who you can count on. For now, don't spend any time identifying an ecosystem.

Next, identify your PEP Team. This is a larger pool of people who would be helpful in an emergency. This list may include co-workers, business partners, professional advisors and extended neighbors, friends and family.

Finally, identify your PEP Team Leaders. These are the folks you will train. Go back to the previous questions and compare it to your list. Who can cover the different aspects of your life? Match your needs to names on your list and determine what roles you want to ask them to perform.

At the very least, should you become incapacitated you need someone to provide care for dependent family members, pets and farm animals, as well as someone to make medical decisions for you, and someone to take care of your finances.

If you are like most married couples, you are relying on your spouse to perform these roles. I highly recommend you have a backup to relieve your spouse. Gerald and I have each other. My daughter is our backup.

Most clients ask their team leaders to perform multiple roles. Do the best you can with the people who are willing to help. Think about the roles you are asking them to do, and provide them with the training to be successful. Will you cross-train your team so they can back up each other?

Give each person the information they need to be successful in the role(s) you want them to perform.

Schedule Your PEP Plan Training Meeting

I suggest hosting the meeting at the same location of your Legacy Drawer so you can review it during the meeting. For most, this will be your home, but I do have several clients who maintain their Legacy Drawer at the office.

If possible, plan a simple meal to enjoy together. *Breaking bread* together is an excellent way to encourage deeper conversations. Express your appreciation for their participation.

Before the meeting, decide how you want to share your PEP Binder. Will you provide them with their own PEP Binder, or show them where your binder is located?

Below is a checklist to prepare for your PEP Plan Training Meeting.

1. Prepare for First PEP Plan Training Meeting

   ____ Who will you invite?

   ____ Will this meeting include a meal?

   ____ Find a date and time that works for you and the majority of your team.

   ____ Follow up with an invitation: email or text will do.

   ____ Purchase gift copies of the *Family Emergency Handbook.*

   ____ If needed, prepare additional copies of your PEP Binder.

   ____ Hand write a thank you card and mail it after the meeting.

2. Tips for a Successful Meeting

   ____ Begin and end on time.

   ____ Keep it simple. A sample agenda includes a warm welcome, overview, and appreciation of attendance. If appropriate, create an agenda to hand out.

   ____ Review/present PEP Binder.

   ____ Review/present Legacy Drawer.

   ____ Break for meal, express your appreciation.

   ____ Encourage discussion and conversation.

   ____ Present gift copies of the *Family Emergency Handbook.*

   ____ Offer to help them with their PEP Plan.

Celebrate! You are a Legacy Builder and setting an example for others to follow.

Maintaining Your Plan

Now that you have created your PEP Plan and celebrated your accomplishment, it's time to create a process for maintaining your Legacy Drawer and PEP Binder.

Create a system that works for you. Without a process to keep information up to date, your plan will quickly become obsolete. Below is how I maintain my plan, but do what works for you.

Although I do my best during the year to update changes as they occur, I miss some. Reviewing the entire plan on an annual basis is an excellent backup plan. There is synergy in attaching the review of the PEP Plan to our tax preparation effort. I review my entire plan while I'm cleaning out my current files. I update our investment accounts with the tax statements we receive in January.

During the year, as each insurance policy renews, I update the insurance section. When it's time to send holiday cards, I update the Communication List.

At the end of the year, I do a life review and set my goals for the next year. I've found this is a good time to schedule two pomodoro sessions to review my End-of-Life Plan and update my draft obituary.

Below are examples of how I updated my records last year:

Section 1: Medical Information

Updated medical history for health changes and surgeries. When we changed doctors, we updated our medical information.

Section 2: Home

When we changed pool companies, we updated the contact list and guest instructions form.

Section 3: Loved Ones

When our dog Lucy got sick, we changed her food and updated her care instructions.

Section 4: Legal Documents

When we updated our legal documents, we cleaned out our Legacy Drawer and updated our contact list.

Section 5: Subscriptions and Security

When we changed how we keep our passwords, we updated this section.

Section 6: Bank Accounts and Credit Cards

When a replacement credit card was received, we updated the Legacy Drawer with a new copy of our cards.

Section 7: Assets

When we sold a truck, we removed the truck's file from the Legacy Drawer.

Section 8: Liabilities

When we paid off a loan, we removed the loan file from the Legacy Drawer and moved it to our current files so it will be with our tax records for the next 7 years.

Section 9: Insurance

As policies renewed, we updated the Legacy Drawer.

Section 10: Personal Information

When I received a new driver's license, I made a copy for the Legacy Drawer and threw the old one away.

Section 11: End-of-Life Plan

I reviewed and updated this file the last week in December.

Section 12: Communication Lists

When I sent holiday cards I updated my contact lists.

Now, it's your turn.

Once you decide how you will maintain your plan, document the process and review it as necessary. In time, maintaining your PEP Plan will become second nature.

Please don't skip this step. Keep the momentum flowing by having a process to keep your information up to date.

Use what works for you, and if you have a better process than my example, I'd love to hear your ideas at

Cindy@CindyArledge.com.

An Invitation

I have one last request. After you have created your own Personal Emergency Preparedness Plan, become an agent of change by:

1. Share what you've learned with others, including me! I'd love to hear your story of how you implemented this plan. I'd love to know what worked, and what would make it even better. My email is Cindy@CindyArledge.com.

2. Buy gift copies of the *Family Emergency Handbook* to share with people you care for.

3. Now is a good time to make a list of the people in your ecosystem. Share this plan with the people who are counting on you and offer to help them create a plan.

4. Recommend the *Be Ready, Life Happens Program* at work.

CONGRATULATIONS!

Creating a PEP Plan reduces PREVENTABLE STRESS.

Give your loved ones the gift of confidence!

Appendix

Family Medical History	70
Home Contact List	71
Guest Instructions	72
Sample Guest Instructions	73
Home Maintenance Checklist	75
Sample Caregiving for Dependents	76
Sample Consent to Treat Dependents	77
Pet Record	78
Farm Animal Record	79
Farm Herd Record	80
Sample POA Pet Emergency Care	81
Sample POA Farm Animal Emergency Care	82
Vital Statistics	83
Advanced Planning and Final Instructions	84
Draft Obituary	86
Time Estimator Sheet	87
Unclaimed Assets	100
Preparing for the Will Conversation	101

Family Medical History For _____ Date Updated: _____

Relationship	Heart Disease	Diabetes	Dementia	Stroke	Cancer (Type)	Other
Father						
Mother						
Maternal Grandmother						
Maternal Grandfather						
Paternal Grandmother						
Paternal Grandfather						
Siblings						

Home Contact List

Date Updated: _____

Location: _____

> Contact information for helpful neighbors, repair service providers, utility companies, maintenance contractors, property managers, preferred real estate agents, home-owner associations, etc.

Guest Instructions

Date Updated:_____

Address: _____

We are so glad you are here!

Your name, telephone number, email address here

Safety first!

Security information:

Description of amenities:

Location of supplies:

Calendar of events:

Care of plants and animals:

Sample Guest Instructions

Welcome to the Ranch!

Address Here
Name / Phone Number

Safety First! This is a rural property, which means there are poisonous snakes, wild critters and biting insects. Be alert. Dress properly. And protect yourself with bug spray and sunscreen. Before getting in the pool, check for snakes and frogs.

Gate Code: XXXX#

Garage Code: Open: XXXX Enter   Close: Enter

Walk-in Door: XXXX (Lock)

Wifi: Wifi name

Wifi Password: XX@aB123

TV Services: AppleTV, Prime Video, Netflix, DVD collection in guest room

The ranch amenities include three bedrooms, four baths, two offices, several covered porches and a deep-water swimming pool. We have fiber optic internet service and various entertainment channels. The guest room has a TV, couch, desk and queen size bed.

The kitchen and pantry are fairly well stocked. There are two refrigerator/freezers: one in the kitchen and one in the garage. Make your own ice with the counter-top ice maker! In addition, there is a small refrigerator in the bar area.

The stove is propane and will automatically light. If you don't hear the clicks, turn the burner off and try again. There is an oven and microwave and two sinks.

Outside, there is a gas grill on the patio. Turn the valve under the grill to the ON position, then use the auto starters to light. Let burners get hot after use, clean with metal brush. Turn burners off, then turn valve off at gas tank after each use. Should the propane run out, there is an extra tank in the barn.

The hot water heater has a timer to deliver hot water faster. You can take a shower/bath at any time, but if you want hot water fast, take your shower/bath between 6:00 and 9:00 in the morning or evening.

Outdoor supplies and paper products are in the garage entryway closet. You will find bug spray, sunscreen and towels, as well as paper towels, toilet paper and paper plates.

Vacuum supplies are located in the closet at the end of the garage entryway. The house has a central vac system, plus there is a portable vacuum cleaner for quick cleanup.

The laundry room is fully stocked with cleaning supplies.

Weekly Calendar:

Monday:

Tuesday: Pool Company

Wednesday:

Thursday: Trash PM

Friday: Bring Trash back

Saturday:

Sunday:

Contact List:

Propane Gas:	Propane gas company	111-222-3333
Septic System:	Septic service company	111-222-3333
Water:	Water service	111-222-3333
Electric:	Electric cooperative name	111-222-3333
Fiber Optic:	Communications company	111-222-3333
Pool:	Pool company	111-222-3333
Vet Clinic:	Vet name	111-222-3333
	Animal names on vet records	

Home Maintenance Checklist

Location: _____   **Date Updated**: _____

	Jan	Feb	Mar	Apr	May	Jun	Jul	Aug	Sept	Oct	Nov	Dec
Change Air Filters												
Change Batteries in Smoke Detector												
Maintain Windows/Doors												
AC/Heater Checkups												
Pool Equipment Checkup												
Sprinkler System Checkup												
Pest Control												
Clean Windows												
Winterize Systems												

Sample Caregiving for Dependents   Date Updated:_____

First Name: _____ Middle Name: _____ Last Name: _____

Date of Birth: _____   Sex: ____

School: _____ Teacher's Name: _____

Address: _____

Contact Information: _____

Authorized to pick up child at school:

1st Designation: _____

2nd Designation: _____

3rd Designation: _____

Contact information for additional resources for providing care:

Contact Information: _____

Assistance to provide: _____

Contact Information: _____

Assistance to provide: _____

Contact Information: _____

Assistance to provide: _____

Contact Information: _____

Assistance to provide: _____

Regular Scheduled Activities:

_____

_____

Legal Guardian: _____ Relationship: _____

Telephone #: Cell: _____ Work: _____

Address: _____

Sample Consent to Treat Dependents

I, _____, parent or legal guardian of _____, born _____, do hereby consent to any medical care and the administration of anesthesia determined by a physician to be necessary for the welfare of my child while said child is under the care of _____ and I am not reasonably available by telephone to give consent.

This authorization is effective from _____ to _____.

_____

Signature of Parent or Legal Guardian

_____

Witness Signature Witness Name (please print)

This consent form should be taken with the child to the hospital or physician's office when the child is taken for treatment.

Family Address _____

Telephone: Father _____ (home) _____ (work)

Telephone: Mother _____ (home) _____ (work)

Child's Birthdate _____

Insurance _____ Policy # _____

Preferred Hospital _____

See attached medical forms to assist in treatment.

Pet Record   **Date Updated:** _____

Pet Name: _____ Breed/Type: _____

Date of birth: _____

Description: _____

Address: _____

General Care Instructions: (feeding schedule, location of food, medications, safety issues)

_____

_____

_____

Food: _____ Purchased from: _____

Medication: _____ Purchased from: _____

Pet Care Providers: (neighbors, veterinarian, pet sitters, day care, lodging, yard cleanup, food and medicine providers)

_____

_____

Instructions for care upon my death:

_____

_____

Instructions for disposition of pet:

_____

Location of ownership papers:

_____

Attach photo here

Farm Animal Record

Date Updated: _____

Name: _____ Breed/Type: _____

Date of birth: _____ Tag #: _____

Description: _____ Value: _____

Address and location: _____

General Care Instructions: (feeding schedule, location of food, medications, safety issues)

_____

_____

_____

Food: _____

Medication: _____

Care Providers: (neighbors, veterinarian, fence repair, feed suppliers, farrier, breeder and potential buyers)

_____

_____

_____

_____

Instructions for care upon my death:

_____

_____

Location of ownership papers:

_____

Attach photo here

Farm Herd Record

Date Updated:_____

Address and location: _____

Name/Tag #	Breed	Color	Date of Birth	Value

General Care Instructions: (feeding schedule, location of food, medications, safety issues)

_____

_____

Food: _____

Medication: _____

Care Providers: (neighbors, veterinarian, fence repair, feed suppliers, farrier, breeder and potential buyers)

_____

_____

Instructions for care upon my death:

_____

Location of ownership papers:

_____

Sample Power of Attorney
Pet Emergency Care

I, Cindy Arledge, owner of record for Lucy, (mixed breed dog), Daisy, (13-year-old Healer) and Bitty Kitty (15-year-old cat) do appoint _____ as my attorney-in-fact, to do all that is necessary or desirable for maintaining the health of Lucy, Daisy and/or Bitty Kitty; specifically, to approve and authorize any and all medical treatment deemed necessary by a duly licensed veterinarian and to execute any consent, release or waiver of liability required by veterinary authorities incident to the provision of medical, surgical or other essential care to my animals by qualified veterinary medical personnel.

This limited power of attorney, goes into effect as of _____ and will cease as of the date I return to home, on or about _____.

_____ may authorize without approval from us veterinary services up to and including $_____; any amounts over and above that will require that he/she or the veterinarian contact me by phone at _____ for discussion and approval.

Regular Vet:

Animal Hospital

Address

City, State, Zip

Phone Number

Emergency/After Hours Vet Clinic:

Emergency Animal Clinic

Address

City, State, Zip

Phone Number

Date: _____ Signed: _____

[pet owner]

Date: _____ Signed: _____

[pet sitter]

Sample Power of Attorney
Farm Animal Emergency Care

I, Cindy Arledge, owner of the farm animals listed on the attached farm record, do appoint _____ as my attorney-in-fact, to do all that is necessary or desirable for maintaining the health and welfare of the animals listed; specifically, to approve and authorize any and all medical treatment deemed necessary by a duly licensed veterinarian and to execute any consent, release or waiver of liability required by veterinary authorities incident to the provision of medical, surgical or other essential care to my animals by qualified veterinary medical personnel.

This limited power of attorney, goes into effect as of _____ and will cease as of the date I return to home, on or about _____.

_____ may authorize without approval from us veterinary services up to and including $_____; any amounts over and above that will require that she or the veterinarian contact me by phone at _____ for discussion and approval.

Regular Vet:

Animal Hospital

Address

City, State, Zip

Phone Number

Emergency/After Hours Vet Clinic:

Emergency Animal Clinic

Address

City, State, Zip

Phone Number

Date: _____ Signed: _____
[owner]

Date: _____ Signed: _____
[authorized agent]

Vital Statistics

Date Updated: _____

First Name: _____ Middle Name: _____

Last Name: _____ Social Security Number: _____

Date of Birth: _____ Birthplace: _____ Sex: ____
                        (city & state or foreign country)

Primary Occupation (before retirement): _____ Years in Practice: ____

Kind of Industry or Business: _____

Marital Status: _____ (married, never married, widowed, divorced, married but separated)

Name of Spouse (use maiden name): _____ Spouse deceased? Yes/No) ____

Last Address: _____

City or Town: _____ State: _____ Zip: _____

County: _____ Phone: _____ Years in County: ____

Race: _____ Of Hispanic or Haitian Origin? Yes ____ No ____
              (If yes, specify: Haitian, Cuban, Puerto Rican, Mexican, etc.)

Highest Grade Completed in School: _____

Immediate Next of Kin: _____ Email Address: _____

    Relationship: _____ Telephone #: _____

    Street Address: _____

    City: _____ State: _____ Zip: _____

Father's Name: (first, middle, maiden, last): _____ State of Birth: _____

Mother's Name: (first, middle, maiden, last): _____ State of Birth: _____

If Veteran: Date of Enlistment: _____ Place of Enlistment: _____

Date of Discharge: _____ Place of Discharge: _____

Serial Number: _____ Rate or Rank: _____

Branch of Service: _____

Advanced Planning and Final Instructions   Date Updated: _____

Empower your family to honor you by communicating your wishes in advance.

____ I have NOT made any plans and want my family to handle any and all my arrangements.

____ I have indicated my wishes below but have not purchased my pre-needs arrangements yet.

____ I have purchased my pre-needs arrangements. Please see attached documents.

After I am gone, please make the following arrangements:

A. Regarding my body (please check one)

____ I wish to be buried. See Funeral Arrangements section below.

____ I wish to be cremated. See Cremation section below.

____ I desire to donate my organs/body. See Donation of Organs/Body section below.

____ I desire alternative arrangements for my body. See Alternative section below.

____ I have no preferences and want my family to make this decision.

Funeral Arrangements (complete all that apply)

____ I have already made pre-arrangement plans at _____.
                                                    (funeral home)

These documents are in my Legacy Drawer which is located at _____.
My executor, _____ (name), has been informed of this plan.

____ I have made arrangements for a headstone at _____ (funeral home).

____ I haven't made burial arrangements yet. I would like my family to retain _____ _____ (funeral home) to handle my funeral.

____ I have a cemetery plot at _____ and I wish to be buried here.

____ I prefer a graveside-only service (in lieu of a memorial or other funeral service).

____ I would like the following people to serve as pallbearers: _____
_____

Cremation (please check one) (Please, know the law before disposing of ashes.)

____ I have already made pre-arrangement plans with _____.
These documents are in my Legacy Drawer which is located at _____.
My executor, _____ (name), has been informed of this plan.

____ I want my ashes scattered at the following location(s) _____.

____ I want my family to retain my ashes.

____ I want my ashes to be made into _____ .

____ I want my family to decide how they want to disperse my ashes.

Donation of organs and/or my body (please check one)

____ I have already pre-arranged plans with _____ that will permit my body parts to be donated for science and/or the benefit of another person. These documents are in my Legacy Drawer which is located _____. My executor, _____ (name), has been informed of this plan.

____ I have not entered into a formal arrangement but would like to donate any part of my body that can be used for science or the benefit of another person.

Alternative Arrangements for my body (insert information here)

____ I have already made pre-arrangement plans with _____. These documents are in my Legacy Drawer which is located _____. My executor, _____ (name), has been informed of this plan.

____ I have not made pre-arrangements but would like the following arrangements to be made_____.

B. Celebration of Life (complete all that apply)

____ I would like donations in lieu of flowers to be made to the following organization: _____.

____ I would like the following flowers to be used: _____.

____ I desire for a memorial service to be held at: _____.

____ I desire for a celebration of life to be held at: _____.

____ I would like the following person to sing at my service: _____.

____ I would like _____ to deliver my eulogy. Their contact information: _____.

____ I would like the following music to be played at my memorial service: _____ _____

____ I would like the following scriptures, prayers, quotes, psalms or poems to be read at my memorial service:

____ I have the following special requests that I would like to have honored:

Draft Obituary

Date Updated: _____

Remember, this is a DRAFT!
Complete in advance to communicate what's important to YOU!

Place photo here

Writing Prompts:

Name:

City of residence:

Age:

Birthdate:

Birthplace:

Favorite smells:

Favorite sounds:

Favorite sights:

What are you most proud of:

Activities and hobbies enjoyed:

How do you want to be remembered?

Preceded by:

Name	Relationship	City/State

Survived by:

Name	Relationship	City/State

In lieu of flowers:

Contributions may be made to (please include address): _____

Contact Person: _____ Telephone: _____

Time Estimator Sheet

If you are not concerned about how long it will take to complete this project, you won't need these forms.

If you are curious about the time commitment, or would benefit from a planning tool, complete the time estimators for each section and record them on the Time Estimator Sheet below.

Remember, a pomodoro session is 25 minutes of working time with a five-minute break. Two sessions equal one hour.

Use the Assignment column to track sections that you can delegate to others.

In the fictional Frye Family story, Heather's initial estimate to complete the PEP Plan was 72.5 hours. This process will take time. Your life is probably more complicated than you realize. The question is: *Are you willing to invest time and effort now to make sure the worst day of your life is a little bit easier?*

Section	Include in PEP Binder	Estimated Hours	Assignment
Medical Information	Yes		
Home	Yes		
Loved Ones	Yes		
Legal Documents	No		
Subscriptions and Security	No		
Bank Accounts and Credit Cards	No		
Assets	No		
Liabilities	No		
Insurance	No		
Personal Information	No		
End-of-Life Plan	No		
Communication Lists	No		
Total Estimated Time	Total		

Medical Section Estimator

Below are the estimated pomodoro sessions to complete the Medical section activities.

Estimated time to complete:

1 pomodoro session per Family Medical History

2 pomodoro sessions per Personal Medical History

1 pomodoro session per Current Medical Condition

2 pomodoro sessions per Medications and Supplements List

2 pomodoro sessions per Medical Equipment and Supplies List

1 pomodoro session per Health Insurance and Veteran's Benefits List

2 pomodoro sessions per Medical Contact List

Use the form below to estimate your time to complete the Medical activities. Record the total number of hours to complete the Medical section on the Time Estimator Sheet.

# of forms	Multiplied by	# of pomodoro sessions	Activity	Total Estimated # of Sessions
	X	1	Family Medical History	
	X	2	Personal Medical History	
	X	1	Current Medical Condition	
	X	2	Medications & Supplements List	
	X	2	Medical Equipment & Supplies List	
	X	1	Health Insurance & Veteran's Benefits	
	X	2	Medical Contact List	
			Total estimated pomodoro sessions:	
			Divide the total pomodoro sessions by 2 to convert to hours.	÷ 2
			Total estimated hours to complete this section: Record on Time Estimator Sheet	

Home Section Estimator

Below are the estimated pomodoro sessions to complete the Home section activities. If you own more than one home, create a separate set of documents for each location. Remember, you will only include homes used for your personal use in this section. It doesn't matter if you are renting or own your home. Whether or not you live in a house, apartment, RV or barn, you have a personal space that needs to be cared for in your absence. If you own rental income properties, you will address rental properties in the Asset section.

<u>Estimated time to complete:</u>

2 pomodoro sessions per Home Contact List

2 pomodoro sessions per Guest Instructions form

1 pomodoro session per Home Maintenance Checklist

1 pomodoro session to file important papers

Use the form below to estimate your time to complete this section. Record the total number of hours to complete the Home section on the Time Estimator Sheet.

# of houses	Multiplied by	# of pomodoro sessions	Activity	Total Estimated # of Sessions
	X	2	Home Contact List	
	X	2	Guest Instructions form	
	X	1	Home Maintenance Checklist	
	X	1	File important papers	
			Total estimated pomodoro sessions:	
			Divide the total pomodoro sessions by 2 to convert to hours.	÷ 2
			Total estimated hours to complete this section: Record on Time Estimator Sheet	

Loved Ones Section Estimator

Below are the estimated pomodoro sessions to complete the Loved Ones section activities.

<u>Estimated time to complete:</u>

1 pomodoro session per Caregiving for Dependents Plan

1 pomodoro session per Consent to Treat Dependents

1 pomodoro session per Pet Record

1 pomodoro session per Farm Animal Record

2 pomodoro sessions per Herd Record

1 pomodoro session per POA Pet Emergency Care

1 pomodoro session per POA Farm Animal Emergency Care

1 pomodoro session per form to file important papers

Use the form below to estimate your time to complete this section. Record the total number of hours to complete the Loved Ones section on the Time Estimator Sheet.

# loved ones	Multiplied by	# of pomodoro sessions	Activity	Total Estimated # of Sessions
	X	1	Caregiving for Dependents Plan	
	X	1	Consent to Treat Dependents	
	X	1	Pet Record	
	X	1	Farm Animal Record	
	X	2	Herd Record	
	X	1	POA Pet Emergency	
	X	1	POA Farm Animal Emergency	
	X	1	File important papers	
			Total estimated pomodoro sessions:	
			Divide the total pomodoro sessions by 2 to convert to hours.	÷ 2
			Total estimated hours to complete this section: Record on Time Estimator Sheet	

Legal Documents Section Estimator

Below are the estimated pomodoro sessions to complete the Legal section activities.

    Estimated time to complete:

    1 pomodoro session to move documents to Legacy Drawer and write a note

    2 pomodoro sessions to copy critical documents

Use the form below to estimate your time to complete this section. Record the total hours to complete the Legal section on the Time Estimator Sheet.

#	Multiplied by	# of pomodoro sessions	Activity	Total Estimated # of Sessions
	X	1	Move documents to Legacy Drawer and write note	
	X	2	Copy critical documents for unsecured Legacy Drawer	
			Total estimated pomodoro sessions:	
			Divide the total pomodoro sessions by 2 to convert to hours.	÷ 2
			Total estimated hours to complete this section: Record on Time Estimator Sheet	

Subscriptions and Security Section Estimator

Below are the estimated pomodoro sessions to complete the Subscriptions and Security section activities.

<u>Estimated time to complete:</u>

2 pomodoro sessions per Subscriptions List

2 pomodoro sessions per Storage and Security List

2 pomodoro sessions per Passwords List

Use the form below to estimate your time to complete this section. Record the total number of hours to complete the Subscriptions and Security section on the Time Estimator Sheet.

# of forms	Multiplied by	# of pomodoro sessions	Activity	Total Estimated # of Sessions
	X	2	Subscriptions List	
	X	2	Storage & Security List	
	X	2	Passwords List	
			Total estimated pomodoro sessions:	
			Divide the total pomodoro sessions by 2 to convert to hours.	÷ 2
			Total estimated hours to complete this section: Record on Time Estimator Sheet	

Bank Account and Credit Card Section Estimator

Below are the estimated pomodoro sessions to complete the Bank Accounts and Credit Card section activities.

Estimated time to complete:

1 pomodoro session per four bank accounts

1 pomodoro sessions per four credit cards

Use the form below to estimate your time to complete this section. Record the total number of hours to complete the Bank Accounts and Credit Cards section on the Time Estimator Sheet.

# of accounts ÷ 4	Multiplied by	# of pomodoro sessions	Activity	Total Estimated # of Sessions
	X	1	Bank Accounts List	
	X	1	Credit Cards List	
			Total estimated pomodoro sessions:	
			Divide the total pomodoro sessions by 2 to convert to hours.	÷ 2
			Total estimated hours to complete this section: Record on Time Estimator Sheet	

Assets Section Estimator

Below are the estimated pomodoro sessions to complete the Assets section activities.

Estimated time to complete:

1 pomodoro session per two assets

2 pomodoro sessions per location to complete a Property Contact List

2 pomodoro sessions per real estate location to set up your property files

1 pomodoro session per other asset to set up your files

Use the form below to estimate your time to complete this section. Record the total number of hours to complete the Assets section of the Time Estimator Sheet.

# of assets	Multiplied by	# of pomodoro sessions	Activity	Total Estimated # of Sessions
	X	1	Asset files	
	X	2	Property Contact List	
	X	2	Property files	
	X	1	Other Asset files	
Total estimated pomodoro sessions:				
Divide the total pomodoro sessions by 2 to convert to hours.				÷ 2
Total estimated hours to complete this section: Record on Time Estimator Sheet				

Liabilities Section Estimator

Below are the estimated pomodoro sessions to complete the Liabilities section activities.

<u>Estimated time to complete:</u>

1 pomodoro session to create a Liabilities List

2 pomodoro sessions per liability to set up your files

Use the form below to estimate your time to complete this section. Record the total number of hours to complete the Liabilities section on the Time Estimator Sheet.

# of liabilities	Multiplied by	# of pomodoro sessions	Activity	Total Estimated # of Sessions
	X	1	Liabilities List	
	X	2	Liabilities files	
			Total estimated pomodoro sessions:	
			Divide the total pomodoro sessions by 2 to convert to hours.	÷ 2
			Total estimated hours to complete this section: Record on Time Estimator Sheet	

Insurance Section Estimator

Below are the estimated pomodoro sessions to complete the Insurance section activities.

<u>Estimated time to complete:</u>

1 pomodoro session to create an Insurance Contact List

1 pomodoro session per policy to set up your files

Use the form below to estimate your time to complete this section. Record the total number of hours to complete the Insurance section on the Time Estimator Sheet.

# of activities	Multiplied by	# of pomodoro sessions	Activity	Total Estimated # of Sessions
	X	1	Insurance Contact List	
	X	1	Policy files	
			Total estimated pomodoro sessions:	
			Divide the total pomodoro sessions by 2 to convert to hours.	÷ 2
			Total estimated hours to complete this section: Record on Time Estimator Sheet	

Personal Information Section Estimator

Below are the estimated pomodoro sessions to complete the Personal Information section activities.

<u>Estimated time to complete:</u>

1 pomodoro session per Vital Statistics form

1 pomodoro session per person to gather and file personal information

Use the form below to estimate your time to complete this section. Record the total number of hours to complete the Personal Information section on the Time Estimator Sheet.

#	Multiplied by	# of pomodoro sessions	Activity	Total Estimated # of Sessions
	X	1	Vital Statistics form	
	X	1	File important documents	
			Total estimated pomodoro sessions:	
Divide the total pomodoro sessions by 2 to convert to hours.				÷ 2
Total estimated hours to complete this section: Record on Time Estimator Sheet				

End-of-Life Section Estimator

Below are the estimated pomodoro sessions to complete the End-of-Life section activities.

<u>Estimated time to complete:</u>

2 pomodoro sessions per Final Instructions form

2 pomodoro sessions per Draft Obituary

1 pomodoro session per Pre-Arrangement Contact List

Use the form below to estimate your time to complete this section. Record the total number of hours to complete the End-of-Life section on the Time Estimator Sheet.

#	Multiplied by	# of pomodoro sessions	Activity	Total Estimated # of Sessions
	X	2	Final Instructions form	
	X	2	Draft Obituary	
	X	1	Pre-Arrangement Contact List	
			Total estimated pomodoro sessions:	
			Divide the total pomodoro sessions by 2 to convert to hours.	÷ 2
			Total estimated hours to complete this section: Record on Time Estimator Sheet	

Communication Section Estimator

Below are the estimated pomodoro sessions to complete the Communication section activities.

Estimated time to complete:

2 pomodoro sessions per Emergency Contact List

2 pomodoro sessions per Personal Contact List

2 pomodoro sessions per Notification of Death List

Use the form below to estimate your time to complete this section. Record the total number of hours to complete the Communication section on the Time Estimator Sheet.

# of lists	Multiplied by	# of pomodoro sessions	Activity	Total Estimated # of Sessions
	X	2	Emergency Contact List	
	X	2	Personal Contact List	
	X	2	Notification of Death List	
			Total estimated pomodoro sessions:	
		Divide the total pomodoro sessions by 2 to convert to hours.		÷ 2
			Total estimated hours to complete this section: Record on Time Estimator Sheet	

Unclaimed Assets

Did you know there is $49 billion of unclaimed assets in the United States?

When my parents passed away it took months to locate all their accounts.

At the time, I didn't know about the National Association of Unclaimed Property Administrators (NAUPA). It is an excellent resource for locating unclaimed assets.

The website is www.unclaimed.org and membership includes 50 state treasurers.

Scroll down and click on your state to conduct your search.

While researching this book, I was curious to see if my husband and I had any unclaimed assets. I am happy to report that we didn't have any.

The site is so fast and easy to use, I searched for several friends and family and found over $1,000 for them.

As you are creating your Legacy Drawer, take a moment to do a search on the unclaimed.org website. Please let me know if you find any lost money!

You can send me a message at Cindy@CindyArledge.com. I'd love to hear your success story.

Preparing for the Will Conversation

A "will" is a group of documents that serves a dual purpose. While you are alive, it protects you, your family, and your "stuff" and empowers "agents" to make decisions for you if you are unable to do so for yourself. Upon your death, it provides legal authority for your agents to wrap up your life and carry out your instructions.

We live in a legal arena. Without legal protection you have abdicated your decisions to state and federal laws. It is an inefficient method that causes UNNECESSARY STRESS, costs more, and takes longer to wrap up your affairs.

Here's some shocking news! You can live through a bad estate plan. I've had seriously ill clients pull through a health crisis to suffer the consequences of being unprepared. The complexity of your life and finances determines the complexity of your "will." This is not a good DIY project. Invest in a quality advisor to provide you with a quality plan.

Follow these simple steps to prepare for the will conversation. Before the meeting:

- Create a current balance sheet showing all assets and liabilities.
- Create a list of personal items that have value or meaning.
- Create a digital asset list of online accounts.
- Check beneficiaries on all insurance policies.
- Check beneficiaries on all bank, investment, retirement, and financial accounts.
- Decide how your estate will be divided. Who are the beneficiaries?
- Decide who will be the executor of your estate. Backup executor?
- Decide who will be the trustee if you have a trust. Backup trustee?
- Decide who will make your medical decisions. Backup?
- Decide who will make your financial decisions. Backup?
- Decide who you will appoint as guardian of minor children. Backup?
- Decide who you will appoint as *your* guardian. Backup?
- Define what quality of life means and make end of life decisions.

Notice: I am not providing legal or financial advice.

Acknowledgments

This book is dedicated to Daisie Smithwick.

I am grateful to the Creator for turning my mess into a message to assist families.

This book is available because of the exquisite expertise of Brian Moreland and Maggie Hicks. You have been with me from the start, and I am thrilled to share this journey with you.

I am thankful to the countless workshop attendees and private clients who helped me refine the process. You know who you are!

It was more difficult than I thought to take workshop material and turn it into a book that empowered readers to complete the process on their own. It sounds weird, but after receiving the first round of edits, I sat with the book for months, just listening to what it wanted to become.

It wanted to be better, so I cut the content in half and sent a second draft to trusted friends, family and respected professional advisors.

I am grateful for the excellent feedback and suggestions from Lauren, Tiffany, Gerald, Niki, Kim, Laura, Nikki, Libbie, Jo, Tylor and countless others who shared valuable input. Thanks to you, this book is ten times better!

Writing this book was an emotional, and often lonely, journey. I couldn't have done it without the loving support of my husband, Gerald, my accountability partner, Sarah, and members of my weekly book club.

Other books by Cindy Arledge

My Camino, My Life

Cur$e of Inheritance

The Legacy Family Way

CRACKING the Inheritance Code

About the Author

CINDY ARLEDGE, MBA brings a fresh new approach to an age-old problem: how to provide your family a financial advantage and avoid ruining their ambition, drive, and relationships to each other.

Motivated by the most painful experience of her life – losing a brother's relationship over a shared inheritance – Cindy developed a process to help business owners preserve family relationships through emotional and financial storms.

While in the *waiting room*, the time between her parents' death and the distribution of their estate, Cindy sought to understand what had happened to her family. In the process, she discovered a growing number of wealthy families who know how to retain wealth for 100 years, and longer.

She was dismayed to discover that 7 out of 10 families lose wealth during the first transfer, and less than 10% retain wealth past the third generation. Shockingly, 97% of the time wealth loss was caused by the family. In other words, *wealth loss* are code words for *family feud*.

Utilizing a lifetime of learning, Cindy crafted a systematic approach to Legacy Planning. She included aspects of spirituality, personal development, psychology, leadership training, financial literacy, best business practices, conscious capitalism and personal experience.

Unlike traditional estate planning, the entire family is invited to participate. The plan is an ongoing process that is established before chaos begins. Cindy's unique ability is simplifying and meshing massive amounts of information from a variety of sources into a practical application to improve the quality of life.

Cindy's original goal was to prevent the pain and suffering she experienced after her parents passed away. Over the years, she has created a repeatable process to live your significant life and empower your family to thrive for generations.

Cindy is a second-generation commercial real estate investment entrepreneur, best-selling author and matriarch of the family. Her vision is to see legacy planning become a recognized industry and help at least one million families.

Cindy's favorite role is that of grandmother, or "Elmo." She enjoys each day as a gift with her husband, Gerald and their four-legged family members. They live in the DFW metroplex where they enjoy time spent with family and friends.